Divine Redirection

Finding Jesus on Your Hard Roads ... and on Every Path Along the Way

By

Billy Huddleston
and
Susie Shellenberger

FaithHappenings Publishers
Centennial, Colorado

Copyright ©2019 by Billy Huddleston and Susie Shellenberger

No part of this publication may be reproduced, distribute, or transmitted in any form or by any means, including photocopying, recording, or other electronic or mechanical methods, without the prior written permission of the publisher, except in the case of brief quotations embodied in critical reviews and certain other noncommercial uses permitted by copyright law. For permission requests, write to the publisher, addressed "Attention: Permissions Coordinator," at the address below.

Printed in the United States of America

Unless otherwise indicated, Scripture quotations are from the ESV® Bible (*The Holy Bible, English Standard Version®*), copyright © 2001 by Crossway. Used by permission. All rights reserved.

Scripture quotations marked HCSB have been taken from *The Holman Christian Standard Bible®* Copyright©1999, 2000, 2002, 2003 by Holman Bible Publishers. Used by permission.

Scripture quotations marked MESSAGE are from *The Message*. Copyright © by Eugene H. Peterson 1993, 1994, 1996, 2001, 2002, 2003. Used by permission of NavPress Publishing Group.

Scripture quotations marked NASB are from *The New American Standard Bible®*. Copyright © The Lockman Foundation 1960, 1962, 1963, 1968, 1971, 1972, 1973, 1975, 1977, 1995, Used by permission.

Scripture quotations marked NCV are from *The Holy Bible, New Century Version*, copyright © 1987, 1988, 1991 by Word Publishing, Dallas, Texas 75039. Used by permission.

Scripture references marked NIV are taken from The Holy Bible, New International Version®, NIV®. Copyright © 1973, 1978, 1984 by Biblica, Inc. Used by permission. All rights reserved worldwide.

Scripture references marked NKJV are from *The New King James Version*. Copyright © 1982, Thomas Nelson, Inc. Used by permission.

Scripture references marked NLT are from *The Holy Bible, New Living Translation*, copyright ©1996, 2004. Used by permission of Tyndale House Publishers, Inc., Wheaton, Ill., 60189 All rights reserved.

All emphases in Scripture have been added by the author.

FaithHappenings Publishing
A division of WordServe Literary
7500 E. Arapahoe Rd. Suite 285
Centennial, CO 80112
admin@wordserveliterary.com
303.471.6675

Cover Design: Tehsin Gull
Interior Book Design: Greg Johnson

First Printing in the U.S.A., September 2019

Dedication

To Madison Busic Shellenberger and
Sarah Ekstrom Shellenberger. You add so very much to our
family! Thank you for your depth, your humor, your solidity
and your love for Jesus.
—Susie

To Anna Ruth Huddleston. I'm blessed to call you my
mom. Thank you for the life you have given me. I love you!
—Billy

Table of Contents

Chapter One: Redirection from the Routine………..............7
Why do we often cling to the familiar when faced with tragedy? The Old Testament prophet Haggai asked the same question. What he discovered could totally rearrange your priorities.

Chapter Two: Redirection from Defeat...…………………..17
A lot can happen in seven days. The two disciples we're joining on the road to Emmaus are barely putting one foot in the front of the other. If you've experienced broken dreams, you'll relate.

Chapter Three: Redirection from Melancholy Music……..29
Meet Asaph—King David's worship leader—whose beautiful music turned sour when he played the comparison game.

Chapter Four: Redirection from a Bad Road Trip………..44
We're catching up with the two disciples on the road to Emmaus. If you've ever had a bad road trip on a beautiful day, you'll fit right in.

Chapter Five: Redirection from Hopelessness…………….60
Ichabod—it's a weird name. His mother allowed their negative environment to determine his identity. Ichabod's best days never even began. This is what it's like to live in hopelessness, and there is absolutely no glory.

Chapter Six: Redirection from Worthlessness……………74
Mephibosheth, like many of us, accepted a label in the place of his name. His story is filled with tragedy, but everything changes when he meets the king.

Chapter Seven: Redirection from a Death Sentence……….89
The tests have been run. The results are in. The doctor calls. The news isn't good. What Naaman has is fatal . . . until he meets the living Remedy.

Chapter Eight: Redirection from Shame………………….103
Something terrible happened to Tamar that wasn't her fault. Though she was the daughter of the king, she lived her life in loneliness. Why? She could have lived in the palace! We sometimes struggle with the same decision.

Chapter Nine: Redirection from Self..........................120
Jacob spent most of his life as a deceiver. It was only when he admitted who he really was that God was able to change his path.

Chapter Ten: Redirection for Tomorrow....................136
We don't know his name, but he spent the last few hours of his life hanging on a cross next to Jesus Christ. In the midst of defeat, ultimate victory was won.

Chapter Eleven: Redirection Becomes Sweet.................152
Let's join the two disciples for dinner in Emmaus. It may surprise you who's serving at this out-of-the-way eatery.

Chapter Twelve: Redirection is a Wonderful Thing.........169
Sometimes the best thing we can do is to admit we're heading the wrong way. It's okay to pause and ask for directions.

Individual and Small Group Study Guide....................180

About the Authors...196

Chapter One
Redirection from the Routine

I loved Jamaica Jane. She was my beautiful golden retriever. She could catch an ice-cube from anywhere in the room. She was graceful and smart and just wanted to make 79I don't know why; I just started cleaning the house like a madwoman. Maybe I needed to throw myself into something routine, mundane . . . something that didn't require thinking.

Years later, my precious 150-lb. St. Bernard, Bosco died. He was a gentle giant—as mellow as the day is long—magnificent to behold. He put himself to bed every single night at 8:15. And yes, he shared my bed. He slept parallel to me with his head on the pillow—just like a human.

Before I had my knee replacement surgery, I remember going to bed on a Saturday afternoon crying. My knees hurt so bad that sleep seemed the only option. So I took a Tylenol p.m. and stretched out on top of the comforter. Lying on my back, with Bosco lying next to me, I cried, "I'm hurting, Bosco. My knees hurt so bad."

Immediately, he stretched his arm across me, trying his best to hug me, to hold me inside the pain. When he died several years later, I once again grabbed the cleaning supplies and moved like a whirlwind throughout my home.

Why?

I don't know. Maybe I was just so heartbroken, I needed to go back to what was familiar—again, searching for the routine, the mundane, doing something that wouldn't require processing my emotions. I gravitated to the familiar.
—**Susie**

Maybe You Can Relate

Haggai knew all about routine. But before we get into that . . . you can't help but smile at his name. Don't you just want to say, "Hey, Guy!" and hear him answer, "Yep. That's me!"

Haggai was a prophet, and he authored a short book in the Old Testament. His book details a group of people who had fallen into routine supreme. Here's the scene:

In 536 B.C., about 50,000 Jews returned from Babylon to Judah. They quickly rebuilt the altar and began offering sacrifices. Two years later, they laid the foundation to rebuild the temple, but opposition from neighboring tribes tempted them to stop the project.

Fast-forward 14 years. The people had become comfortable with routine: They were busy farming, building houses, having families, living life.

> The book of Haggai is the second shortest book in the Old Testament.

Because they had fallen into the convenient standard of everyday activity, they'd become used to life without a temple. They grew content with their routine. They lost their vision, and God's house was no longer a priority.

Maybe you can relate. Perhaps you made a commitment to Christ. You were excited to serve Him. You couldn't wait to open your Bible and spend time in the Word. You prayed often. You were involved in church. You went to a Bible study. You were actually growing stronger in Christ.

But something happened.

You faced opposition.

You took the wrong exit.

Someone dampened your enthusiasm.

You got hurt.

You experienced trials that God didn't remove even after you prayed He would.

You lost your spiritual vision.

Bills mounted.

You let your employer schedule extra hours for you to work—even though it was a Sunday shift.

You still go to church—when you can—but it's no longer the extreme center of your life. You tell others that you just don't have the time to serve as you used to. You're not deliberately rebelling against God, but you've slowly put your house above God's house.

You've become comfortable with a methodical standard of living. You can relate to the people of Haggai's day.

It's inside this scene of routine that God raises up Haggai as a prophet. Sometimes we need to be reminded that routine isn't always a good thing. Haggai was the living reminder.

He confronted the people with tough questions: **"Why is everyone saying it is not the right time for rebuilding my Temple?"** asks the Lord.

His reply to them is this: **"Is it then the right time for you to live in luxurious homes, when the Temple lies in ruins? Look at the result: You plant much but harvest little. You have scarcely enough to eat or drink and not**

enough clothes to keep you warm. Your income disappears, as though you were putting it into pockets filled with holes!" (Haggai 1:2-6 LB)

Haggai directed their attention to the fact that they were working overtime to make ends meet, but they still never had enough money. They had neglected the temple because the routine of life had become more important.

When routine becomes more important than God's calling on our lives . . .

When routine shifts to paramount and our spiritual vision is reduced . . .

When routine emerges more significant than God's commands . . . we're outside of His will.

Rachel decided to break the routine and did something her family didn't expect. Here's her story:

Rachel gave her heart to Christ when she was a little girl. "He has always been so faithful and kind to me," she says. "When I was just 14 years old, I felt God's call to missions."

Most of Rachel's family members are dedicated Christians, but none of them is in fulltime ministry, so this announcement from a teenager was hard for them to accept. After all, she could certainly be a strong Christian and serve God in a variety of places like millions of others do. But fulltime ministry? Why break her family routine? No one else was involved in career ministry.

"My announcement was simply shrugged off," Rachel says, "and everyone assumed I'd go to college and become a teacher or a writer. And after a while, I even started to buy into that. It's what made sense."

Rachel's dad works at the state university, so tuition for her would be free. "I attended my first year there and was miserable," she says. "It wasn't because I didn't like the school or the subject matter; it just didn't feel right to me. I knew there had to be more."

Her parents couldn't help but notice how unhappy she was and told her that she could apply to some ministry schools. But they told her she could only attend if one of those other colleges could give her a full scholarship since she could attend college for free by staying local.

The Impossible Dream

"This seemed impossible to me," Rachel says. "My grades were good, but my test scores weren't full-ride material. Still, in the midst of the doubt, I could see God working and adding to the faith I already had. It was exciting, and I was ready to leave the routine of staying at home."

Rachel began her search, and by April of her freshman year, she stumbled on Central Bible College in Springfield, Missouri. "I'd heard about it," she says, "but I honestly never considered it. After all, Missouri was a long way from my home state of Ohio."

> When routine becomes more important than God's calling on our lives, we're outside of His will.

As she viewed their scholarship page, she read that one full scholarship was given each year to incoming students. She grinned when she noticed that her test scores were good enough to qualify for application.

"Time was running out," Rachel says. "I only had a couple of weeks to apply for the school and the scholarship. I was scared. I had no idea what I was getting myself into, but God assured me that He was in this."

She prayed over the envelope containing her application before dropping it into the mailbox. "I told Jesus that I wanted to be in the center of His will. My utmost desire was obedience," Rachel says.

Deep in her heart, she had decided that she'd move to Springfield and attend CBC no matter what, but she prayed that God would touch her parents' hearts and move them to know this was His will.

"I knew that without this scholarship there would be a lot of stress on my family, a lot of arguments, and a lot of debt. I didn't want that, but I knew beyond a doubt that God was in this. I couldn't turn away from it."

Divine Direction

Though Rachel thought it seemed highly unlikely she'd get the scholarship, she continued to pray for the sake of her parents. During Fourth of July weekend—less than a month before she would be moving—Rachel received a phone call from an administrator informing her that she had been chosen for the scholarship.

"I cried on the phone with him," she says. "I was so overwhelmed at God's goodness! He had heard and answered my prayer. He truly interrupted my routine and divinely directed me right inside of His will. Not only would I attend debt-free, but I'd be in an environment conducive to missions work, and He had provided confirmation for my family.

"I felt God was telling me and my family once and for all that He had called me and we were never to question that again," she says. "And *because* He has called, He will be faithful to meet my needs. *My* responsibility," Rachel says, "is to trust, obey, and follow even when the steps are risky and don't seem to make sense."

A few years later, Rachel again allowed God to disrupt her comfortable routine. She moved across the nation to Seattle—without a car, a job, or a place to live—to help with a church plant. Within a month, she had secured a job as a nanny with a family that has become like a second family to her. "More than once, God has provided all I've needed in His perfect timing," she says.

God's Interruption

After helping get the new church plant grounded, God interrupted Rachel's routine again. "It was completely out of my comfort zone," she says, "but God moved me to Guadalajara, Mexico where I'm now teaching preschool.

"This is the joy and beauty of life lived with Christ! It's one big, wonderful adventure—IF we allow Him to keep directing and redirecting our steps. If we hold onto our comfortable routine, we'll never experience all He has in store for us. My life with Him is far more amazing than what I ever could have planned on my own!"

***

Do What's Right

Would the people to whom Haggai was speaking allow God to break *their* routine? Haggai was a terrific motivational speaker. But even the best communicators can't move what's not there. Though his words were powerful—and straight from God—he couldn't produce the desire in their hearts to do what was right.

And this is where things get extremely interesting.

His people admitted they had no desire to rebuild the temple. Even though things weren't great, they were comfortable with how they were.

So Haggai basically told them that obedience should outweigh desire. Most of us have it backward. We pray, "God, give me the desire to read the Bible."

"Lord, help me want to share my faith."

"Jesus, move me to get up and go to church."

What if you simply obeyed Him in spite of the absence of desire?

Tithe even though you don't want to release 10 percent of your income. Pray when you want to sleep. Read your Bible though the checkbook needs to be balanced.

> Obedience should outweigh desire.

Obey God anyway.

Popular singer Martina McBride wrote the song "Anyway."

God is great, but sometimes life ain't good

When I pray it doesn't always turn out like I think it should

But I do it anyway

I do it anyway

Because of copyright laws, we're limited to the small amount of lyrics we can reprint here, but go to YouTube and search for it. Listen to the words. The theme rings clear: Do what's right—even when you don't feel like it.

***

I love going to Dan and Becky's for dinner. We laugh, enjoy good food, and Becky always has Coca-Cola for me. Great friends and great times.

I remember a specific time when I left late. The streets were dark, and I walked around the corner to where I had parked my car. Space was limited and a few other cars were close to mine. I gently backed up from the curb to veer into the street and immediately heard the sickening *crunch* of hitting the car behind me.

I quickly got out to see what I'd done and though it was minimal, I knew a body shop would need to replace the bumper of the car I hit.

A fleeting thought entered my mind.

It's dark. No one saw me.

I immediately dismissed the thought. I would do the right thing. Even though my stomach had a knot the size of the Grand Canyon, I grabbed a piece of paper and wrote the following note:

"My name is Susie Shellenberger. I accidentally hit your car when backing up. I'm so sorry. Here's my phone number. Call me so I can take care of the damage."

Sigh.

I couldn't afford whatever it would cost to fix the damage I had just caused.

Temptation offered a quick escape. But I had to do the right thing. I didn't *feel* like doing the right thing, but I was committed to do it anyway.

I've never regretted being obedient to God's ways.

--Susie

Haggai's people decided to do the right thing. They obeyed God even though they had no desire to rebuild the temple. And guess what happened! *After* they began the building process, the desire came!

So Where's MY Roadmap?
Did you catch that?

It's easy to miss if we're not careful.

After they put into action what they knew was right, they discovered redirection. The right exit never looked so good. Routine became extraordinary. God's clarity flooded onto their lives like a brand-new GPS. That's worth celebrating.

That's great for Haggai's people, you may be thinking. *But I need more than a story from the Old Testament.*

That's fair. Let's mingle with the disciples.

Wait a minute. They're extraordinary. I need some everyday people I can relate to.

Yes, the disciples eventually lived and acted in God's supernatural power, but it wasn't always that way. Like the people in Haggai's day, they too almost drowned in defeat. They sought escape through the routine of familiar.

After you've finished the study section on page 181, we'll walk with two disciples on a very familiar road.

Chapter Two
Redirection from Defeat

Everyone loves a good road trip—and this one started with a great idea. Don't most road trips begin this way?

"The year was 1971," Tyler says. "Disney World had just opened in Orlando, Fla., and my family was living in Woodward, Okla.—the panhandle of the state.

"My parents decided to take my sister and me to visit the new theme park that summer. As a 9-year-old, I couldn't imagine anything better! My 4-year-old sister and I helped load the car, and we launched into the 20-and-a-half-hour family road trip."

Though Tyler's dad was exhausted from driving, he was even more frustrated when he pulled the car onto the road in Orlando leading to Disney World.

"The car line to even get inside the parking lot was so long, my dad simply said, 'Nope, I'm not waiting in that line.' He immediately turned our car around and drove back home! To this day—as a mom with two daughters—I've never been to Disney World."

***

It's amazing how quickly things change. Twenty hours earlier a family of four was headed in the right direction for an exciting vacation. Twenty hours later, the dream was killed.

Tyler's dad returned to the familiar.

***

The disciples understood returning to familiarity. It was only a week ago . . . everything seemed to be in place.

All the pieces fit.

Blind received their sight.

Lepers were cleansed.

Even the dead had breathed again.

Yes, it seemed Jesus was establishing His Kingdom. Soon the Jews would be free from Roman rule, and the Messiah would reign on earth. Exactly who would sit at His right and left hand was yet to be decided. The disciples had argued about it—each supposing he was in the running—but Jesus interrupted the heated discussion by pulling a child onto His lap and focusing on servant hood.

OK. The disciples could figure out the royal order later. Nothing could remove the excitement of actually seeing the long-awaited promise being fulfilled before their eyes.

But that was a week ago.

A lot can happen in seven days.

A bitter betrayal.

Six trials. A cross. Excruciating torture. Then death.

It was over.

He was dead.

The Savior had failed to save Himself.

Jesus was gone. The One in whom they'd placed their trust, their hopes, and their dreams was now out of the picture.

And out of their lives.

The Cross punctured the promise.

The disciples invested everything in Him—including eternity.

The tomb was sealed.

Angels wept, and demons danced.

Roman soldiers stood guard. And the disciples scattered.

Moving Slowly

We have twenty-six letters in our alphabet, but we only need one to begin the description of the disciples at this moment: *D*.

    Deflated.

        Dejected.

            Discouraged.

                Defeated.

New direction needed?

Definitely. But even that's an absurd understatement.

Feet that once followed in the footsteps of their Teacher were now dragging a path of their own. They had traveled a road that led to an exciting new world, a bright future. It was the *right* road.

But today it seemed mundane, maybe even meaningless—because they were headed in the *wrong* direction. With not even a wisp of hope to cling to, the disciples went back to how life used to be. Back to where it all began. They were headed away from the Promise.

Isn't this exactly where many of us find ourselves when we're in the midst of defeat? The sweetness of life that we once enjoyed seems nowhere on the horizon . . . so just like the disciples, we gravitate to the familiar.

The disciples, too, craved the familiar. Were their thoughts the same as ours when we lose someone or something dear?

What do I do now?

What's next?

Move.

Put one foot in front of the other. Find the routine. Seek the familiar. Maybe there I'll find comfort.

> Beware: The familiar can easily be an escape that keeps us from having to process the immediate.

Peter, the fisherman extraordinaire, headed back to his boat and grabbed his fishing gear. A few other disciples sought the company of each other. Some stayed inside their homes. All felt abandoned and hopeless. All sought the comfort of routine.

Often that's helpful. *But beware: The familiar can easily be an escape that keeps us from having to process the immediate.*

The Two

Though we don't know a tremendous amount about them, they have a reputation in Christian circles. They're known as "the two who walked the road to Emmaus."

Let's read how Luke introduces them:

"Now that same day two of them were going to a village called Emmaus, about seven miles from

Jerusalem. They were talking with each other about everything that had happened." (Luke 24:13-24 NIV)

Later, in verse 18, we'll discover one of these two is a man named Cleopas. The Bible never gives us the name of his companion, so it must not be important in understanding their story. Though they're not among the 12, these were two of the many disciples of Jesus.

We can see from Luke's GPS which direction these two are headed. They're leaving Jerusalem and walking toward Emmaus. Though it reads like an ordinary journey in the beginning, it actually started to feel like a bad trip nightmare as soon as they left Jerusalem. Like Tyler's dad, these guys were exceedingly defeated. They were ready to quit.

***

I can identify. Not too long ago, I wrestled with wanting to quit. I'm a fulltime evangelist. I travel 48 weeks each year and open God's Word to church congregations across the nation. My summers are filled with family camps. A lot of people spend their vacation in a Bible camp environment with friends from their own church joining with other churches for a week of teaching, preaching and outdoor activities.

These camps can be exhilarating. Seven days of focused attention on Christ and becoming spiritually

> The disciples invested everything in Him—including eternity.

recharged is definitely a great way to spend a vacation. It was mid-August, and though I was enjoying the time of ministry, I admit I was physically and emotionally drained.

This particular camp was 10 days. We met in an outdoor building and had three services a day. Because the temperatures were near 100 degrees, I was preaching to people who seemed to be in a heat coma. Their response was understandably lacking.

One night during the week I lay in bed in my primitive surroundings and let my mind wander. My thoughts chased the question: *What else could I be doing besides preaching?*

I was ready to quit. Though my degree is in religion, and I've been preaching for more than 20 years, when I'm tired I start to feel defeated.

My degree isn't worth much outside the church. What else am I qualified to do? Sure, I could sell cars. I could grab an entry-level management position somewhere. Or maybe I could become a motivational speaker. But my calling . . . and my heartbeat has always been to preach God's Word.

I knew that.

But again, I was drained. My exhaustion was getting the best of me. I was moody and had lost sight of where I needed to be. I'm sure that my attitude affected the way that I delivered the message those last few days. My current melancholy not only impacted my personal life, but also my responsibility to the camp, campers and call. I had forgotten that my attitude would have an impact on all those things. Thankfully, God began to show me I was focused on the wrong things. Deep in my heart I knew quitting wasn't the answer. My responsibility wasn't only to God and myself . . . but to others as well. Sometimes we fail to appreciate the impact our choices have on others. I *knew* that. But what I *knew* and what I *felt* were in a battle during the midnight darkness.

Then I remembered.

The Old Testament prophet Elijah felt the same way.

He had just won the "Battle of the Bulls" held at Mount Carmel Arena. God had unequivocally displayed Himself in a fire that consumed a bull on the altar. Empowered with God's strength, Elijah miraculously defeated 450 false prophets who were serving the idol Baal.

Queen Jezebel was furious and vowed to kill him. So naturally, Elijah ran for his life and hid in the mountains. And tucked between the rocks and the hills, he told God he was ready to quit.

Actually, Elijah told God he wanted to die. I imagine him in primitive surroundings even worse than mine, shaking his head and whispering, "I've had it. I'm done. I can't go on."

Tough situation?

You bet. And it reeked of defeat.

That's exactly where I was. Maybe you've been there, too.

Instead of responding, "I've had it with you, Elijah!" God responded in kindness and gave Elijah exactly what he needed: a nap and some food.

I like that.

And it was exactly what my drained mind and exhausted body needed: solid sleep and great food. Several days of this can be healing.

I didn't quit. And I don't intend to. —**Billy**

***

Back to the Disciples

Luke has tracked them on the road to Emmaus, seven miles outside of Jerusalem. How long would it take to walk seven miles? Aside from Usain Bolt—who has been tagged as the fastest person in the world—the average human can walk three miles in an hour.

But these disciples were defeated, so they probably walked at a slower pace. It could have easily taken them a little more than three hours. Settle in. We're joining them. But due to space in this book, we promise it won't take three hours to get where they're going.

Scripture tells us they were talking about what had happened. What was that? It was Christ's death and resurrection.

Let's set the scene.

History tells us it's Sunday afternoon.

The main topic of conversation in Jerusalem is the execution of Christ. The week had been filled with controversy, illegal trials and a dash of mystery. Against the backdrop of Christ's torturous death, a new twist has risen . . . risen straight from the tomb.

Sure enough, His body was missing.

Jerusalem is buzzing with the news. Or was it merely gossip? The two disciples aren't sure. But one thing they *do* know is the fact that Jesus died on a cross.

And these two men are living within that defeat.

They're dragging their feet on a dusty road outside of Jerusalem. They're leaving the city of hope and heading into darkness.

They've had it.

They're quitting.

What will we do now?
What's the point of going on?
It was silly to put our hope in Him.
Defeat?
Undeniably.

Chris was so familiar with defeat, he began wondering if it was his middle name. He was single and on staff in a 200-hundred-member church and loved his role as visitation, discipleship and prayer pastor. The older people especially loved him because he served with such tenderness. It was easy to sense his love and genuine concern with every conversation. He made several hospital calls each day, but he also spent quite a bit of time in the office to meet with people who stopped by the church for counsel or prayer.

Chris also enjoyed the times his senior pastor asked him to preach during his absence. "Like all churches, this one had its share of problems—people vying for control, some wanting the senior pastor to move on and a younger one to replace him, and so on," Chris says.

Chris is a peacemaker and tried his best to calm those who created conflict, but trouble multiplied quickly. "I felt defeated," he says. "I did everything I could to bring people together, but things often just blew up in my face."

The pastor resigned and conflict increased. A new pastor arrived, and Chris assumed things would get better, but the new minister felt led to take the church in a different direction, and the situation only became more intolerable. Chris resigned.

"While all this was happening at the church, my grandmother—living in another state—was close to death, and my parents were also in extremely poor health. After much prayer, I heard God telling me to go home—where my parents and grandmother lived—several states away," he says.

It would take almost all of his personal savings to move himself across the nation, and though he had no job once he arrived, he knew he was in the center of God's will.

He found a small one-bedroom apartment and immediately began applying for ministry positions while helping care for his parents and grandmother. "I didn't think it would take long at all to find ministry work," he says. "I had a great resume with wonderful experience, but I kept running into dead-ends."

With money running low, he began applying for secular jobs. "I just needed something to make rent until I could find a ministry job, so I was willing to take anything—flipping burgers, waiting tables, you name it."

Though he was *willing* to do anything, employers felt he was too talented for many of the jobs he was applying for, so he wasn't even able to get a job at burger joints. Months passed, and Chris had used almost all of his savings.

> It's important to recognize that defeat doesn't have to be final.

Feeling Defeated

"I knew God had brought me here, but I really needed Him to affirm I was in the center of His will. I have to admit, I felt defeated. Why couldn't I find work? How would I pay rent?"

Chris not only needed rent money; he also had to make his car payment—along with insurance—so he began selling his furniture. He sold his TV, couch and dining room table and was finally down to the bare essentials, but he still didn't have a job.

"I continued to apply to every place available," he says. "I couldn't believe I wasn't getting *anything*. I mean, you just assume you can always get a job flipping burgers somewhere! I don't ever remember feeling that low in my life."

After eight months without a job, Chris had done all he could do. "At the end of another month, I knew I'd be living in my car," he says. "I had no more money for rent; I'd sold everything I could. I had applied for every possible job I could find—yet I still didn't have work."

Though Chris felt like he was living in defeat, he continued to focus on God's faithfulness thus far in his life. "He has never let me down . . . but I was about to be homeless," he says.

Turning Around

Nine months after Chris had moved across the nation to help care for his loved ones, a church 30 minutes away offered him the position of senior pastor. "Talk about perfect timing! I didn't have the money to stay one more day in my apartment. This church has a parsonage that I now live in—and they just did some amazing remodeling to it! So I'm out of apartment life with an actual home, and I'm in a church filled with people who love me and are excited about growing in Christ. God has never failed me. Life isn't always easy, but He never let me go hungry, and He has always met my needs. When I thought I'd hit a dead-end, God turned me around in the right direction."

***

Chris knows what defeat feels like. And the two disciples on the road to Emmaus are *living* in it. Do you sense what they're experiencing? Maybe you've been there. It's hard to take a step forward when defeat leaves you crippled.

It's important to recognize that defeat doesn't have to be final. In the midst of struggle this reality can be lost. The battle steals the hope of victory and we are consumed. We are tempted to believe we're alone and that this is all that will ever be. Struggles will come. So will defeat. Just remember—it's only part of our story. Soon, another page will be written.

The disciples are disillusioned. Everything has fallen apart. They are journeying in defeat. But Luke doesn't end the story here. In fact, this is only the beginning. These two men are about to have a life-changing encounter that will alter their personal history.

Right now, we'll leave them in the middle of the road. We'll come back and join them in a bit. Consider completing the study section on page 182, we'll meet someone else who knows the necessity of divine redirection. For him, it came in the genre of a melancholy tune. Perhaps you'll recognize the sound.

Chapter Three
Redirection from Melancholy Music

I don't like admitting this, but it's easy for me to feel defeated.

I've often joked with God asking if I wear Him out.

I seriously love what I do. There's nothing I enjoy more than opening the Bible to groups of people. As a fulltime speaker, I get to do this 43 weeks or weekends each year. I speak in churches, at family camps, women's conferences, on university campuses and dog parks. OK, I'm kidding about the dog park, but I *do* enjoy taking Amos and Bentley there for a good run.

I was speaking at a "women-in-ministry" retreat in Oregon. The weather was gorgeous, Oregon is always beautiful, and the women were excited about God's calling on their lives. It was every speaker's dream. God anointed our sessions and moved in the lives of those precious ladies. I was leaving on a spiritual high.

I arrived at the Eugene airport about an hour and a half before my flight was scheduled to depart. But when I got to the ticket counter to check in, I was told my flight had already left. The airline had changed the departure time and had failed to inform me.

This specific airline had always done a great job at texting or emailing me whenever there was a change in flight plans, but for some reason this time they didn't.

The man behind the counter checked all the other airlines that flew out of the Eugene airport and told me they couldn't get me home until the next afternoon. I called the airline. After putting me on hold for almost half an hour, they told me the same thing and apologized for not letting me know about the change in departure.

I had to take a late flight to San Francisco then an all-night flight to Chicago. The next day, I caught a flight from Chicago to my home in Oklahoma City.

Yes, I got home . . . a day later.

Yes, my luggage arrived with me.

But sitting alone in the Eugene airport, I lost it.

I was emotionally drained from speaking at several sessions during the weekend. I was physically exhausted and fighting a respiratory infection.

So, I told God I'd had it. I did *not* want to spend the night in an airport or on an airplane.

"There has to be an easier way for me to tell people about You," I said. "Don't get me wrong, Lord. I'm grateful I'm not sitting in the bottom of a muddy well like Jeremiah. And I'm glad I haven't been beaten, shipwrecked and stoned like Paul. But right here right now, I just want to throw in the towel on this whole speaking and traveling thing. I want to be home, in my own bed and with my two dogs."

God allowed me to have my meltdown.

He even gave me a solid night's sleep on the all-night flight.

And when I arrived in the Chicago airport, I got a great breakfast at McDonalds. And after I arrived home and took a shower . . . three days later (my hot water tank broke while I was gone), I started to feel normal again.

I'm grateful that God understands my mood swings. He's so faithful to hold me, let me cry and minister to me when I'm depleted. In chapter two, Billy shared about a time he felt like throwing in the towel. I guess that's why we both identify with the man you're about to meet. —**Susie**

***

His name is Asaph.

He had a special calling on his life.

He was a worship leader.

Asaph was from the Levite tribe. Years earlier, when God freed the Israelites from being Pharaoh's slaves, He set the tribe of Levites apart for ministry. And Moses was obedient to only choose priests from that specific tribe.

So here's the bottom line: If you didn't have Levi ~~jeans~~ . . . genes . . . you couldn't be in a ministry position.

Glad you're paying attention.

Back to Asaph.

We can assume as a Levite, he was wearing the right jeans, because he carried the prescribed genes. He had an extremely important role in ministry.

> Every time we replace worship with comparison . . . we head the wrong direction.

Asaph had actually been appointed by King David to be his music director. He was in charge of the temple music. This is where the Ark of the Covenant dwelled. So Asaph had an important job in an important place among important things and important people. He was called to usher in the presence of God with his worship. That's a high calling.

Historians tell us Asaph was probably in his 20s when he began this specific role. He served in Jerusalem during King David's entire reign and set many of David's psalms to music. Asaph even wrote 12 psalms of his own (Psalms 50, 73-83).

Asaph heard David announce that his son Solomon would someday reign in his place, build the Temple, and establish a kingdom that would remain forever. He witnessed David's death, saw Solomon take the throne and watched the building of the Temple.

What a great time to be in ministry and in the center of God-blessed economic and spiritual growth. Asaph was certainly living a mountaintop life. By pushing the fast-forward button, however, we see his mountaintop soon crumble. His beautiful song turned melancholy.

Asaph saw Solomon's great beginning slide into a nasty decline. His heart grieved at Solomon's wicked pursuit of power, wealth, women and luxury. We can only imagine how heart-broken Asaph was when Solomon began oppressing the people and turning them into slaves to feed his personal greed.

The same Solomon who asked God to give him wisdom to rule, soon turned his back on that wisdom and worshiped the idols of his numerous wives. And Asaph noticed.

It Happens Every Time

As a worship leader, Asaph knew God was the true object of praise. And as long as he directed his attention to the Giver of music, he was captured in genuine worship.

His song was magnificent.

Harmonious melody infused with brilliance.

Notes impeccably orchestrated in genius.

Perfectly synthesized rhythm wrapped itself through his being.

Asaph lived the song.

The aria was his breath.

Until.

Until he shifted his attention from God to people.

That's when his melody turned melancholy.

He lost his way.

And it happens every. single. time.

Whenever we look to people instead of God . . . every time we replace worship with comparison . . . we head the wrong direction.

***

Shane accepted the position of youth pastor in a 300-member church when he was 21. "I was young, driven and ready to set the world on fire," he says. "I couldn't wait to get to church each day and jump into planning and programs and growing the youth group. I was excited about putting into practice what I'd learned in ministry classes."

It seemed as though Shane was doing everything right. The youth group exploded. Students were drawn to him and quickly responded to his outgoing personality. "God began to bless our growth," he says.

But Shane wasn't satisfied. "I saw other youth groups with bigger budgets and plans and was envious when I saw students flocking to larger churches. I quickly became greedy. I wanted a *bigger* youth group. I wasn't happy with a good program; I became obsessed with having the best youth group in town. I wanted extravagant activities; I wanted everything to be maxed-out."

Flashy programs may work for a while, but when ministry is wider than it is deep, trouble begins to brew. "I began comparing myself with the senior pastor, and because I was getting bigger numbers in our youth group than he was pulling into the adult mid-week service, I decided I was the better leader and should be in charge."

The pastor who had tried to mentor Shane began to see that the youth pastor he had hired had become a time bomb in the comparison game. "I became almost manic in my drive to do more, be more and produce more. I started influencing my youth leaders to think that we could do much better by splitting off and planting our own church."

Several people jumped on Shane's bandwagon, but as the time drew closer to actually leave the church, things fell apart. "Our numbers in the youth group dropped, people left, and the leaders I had convinced to move with me decided to stay."

Shane torpedoed into a downward spiral. "I ignored everything I was brought up on," he says. "I knew God desired to help me, but I wanted things done my way." By the time he turned 24, he had lost it all. "Everything came unglued," he says. "The youth group fell apart, I lost my church, my fiancé left, and of course I lost my job. And to top it off, I was robbed at 3 a.m. in the night."

The intruders held a gun to Shane's head, and during the moments he stared into the barrel, he immediately saw God at work. "I felt as though I heard Him say, 'Do I have your attention now?' And He most certainly did!

"I believe God used that unfortunate robbery to wake me up spiritually. He opened my eyes. I realized that I had been operating totally out of myself and not in His will or in His power."

Four years later, Shane is now married to the fiancée who left him. When she saw the change in his surrendered life, she was attracted to Shane's genuine spiritual growth.

> God wants to enable us to remain faithful in the *midst* of trials.

"Right now, I'm a volunteer with the youth program at our church in Columbus, Ohio, but I'm not on staff. I also play the guitar with the worship team, and I help with a few other ministries in the church. My wife and I are carefully seeking God's guidance. Our desire is to be in fulltime ministry, but we definitely want it to be His perfect will and in His perfect timing. I don't care if He gives me a big ministry or a small one—I just want to be in the center of His will. I'm finished playing the comparison game."

***

No One Wins

When we compete in the comparison game, we play a battle that offers pride as its trophy. In pride, we rejoice that we're not like "that guy" (remember the Pharisee in Luke 18:9-14), or we feel sorry for ourselves thinking we'll never be good enough, or we convince ourselves that we're better than those around us. The pride trophy sports an interesting figurine: a person headed in the wrong direction.

Asaph almost became obsessed with the wickedness surrounding him. We understand. We, too, live in a wicked world, and it's easy to become deceived. In fact, we've hurled some of the same questions to God that he launched. Let's look straight inside his personal journal:

> "[The wicked] have nothing to worry about, not a care in the whole wide world. The wicked get by with everything; they have it made, piling up riches."
> (Psalm 73:4, 12 NIV)

Asaph noticed something that many of us have also struggled with: *Why do ungodly people seem to prosper? I'm serving You, God, so why are they getting blessed and I'm not?*

He sees that things easily go their way, and he's deeply disturbed—almost to the point of throwing in the towel—as we'll soon read. It's one thing to be troubled; it's another thing to be obsessed.

Asaph is waving the pride trophy, and it will bring him to the lowest point in his life. As we continue to read his journal (in verses 4-5 from the NIV), we can't help but notice his bewilderment:

> "[Not only do they] have no struggles; their bodies are healthy and strong. They are free from common human burdens; they are not plagued by human ills."

Why am I down with the flu and they never seem to get sick? They don't struggle with the same problems as everyone else. They don't have a care in the world.

Asaph is not only headed in the wrong direction; he's wallowing in the potholes on the road. Again, no one wins in the comparison competition. He's going so far in the wrong direction he has discarded the map. Here's his journal entry found in Psalm 73:13-14 from The Message:

> "I've been stupid to play by the rules; what has it gotten me? A long run of bad luck, that's what—a slap in the face every time I walk out the door."

Perhaps you've entered something similar in your own journal. When inside this kind of pit, it can be hard to climb out.

But though Asaph is struggling internally, he recognizes his responsibility to his community, so he refrains from exploding on others:

> "If I'd have given in and talked like this, I would have betrayed your dear children."

Asaph is close to giving up. Here's his journal entry:

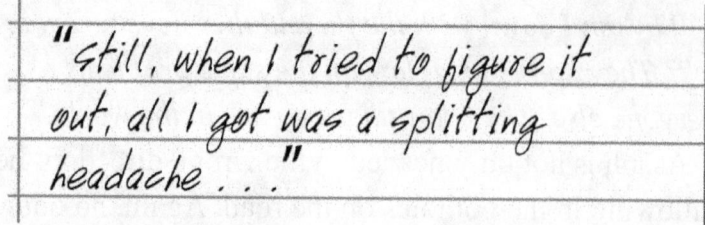

"Still, when I tried to figure it out, all I got was a splitting headache..."

He's so confused, he can't think straight. This is what happens when we continue to take the wrong exit.

But wait a minute. Something's happening.

Asaph turns the corner.

Notice the first word in verse 17 of his journal entry:

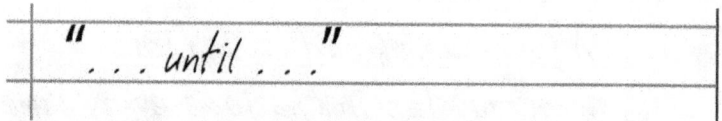

"...until..."

This one word pushes the gearshift in his thinking from reverse to forward!

"...until I entered the sanctuary of God."

(Psalm 73:17 The Message)

Ahhhh.

This is where we find the sweetness of God.

There is always divine redirection in God's sanctuary.

Where is your sanctuary? Do you have a private place that you enjoy meeting with God? A "war room"? The Old Testament prophet Habakkuk had a watchtower. You may have a favorite room in your home, or a loved and well-worn recliner. Perhaps you like to cozy up on a big couch.

We all need a sanctuary where we can shut out all distractions and truly hear from God. This is how we find redirection. This is when the Holy Spirit ministers to us in a deep bone-marrow kind of way.

Let's keep reading his journal:

> "then I understood their end."
>
> (Psalm 73:17 NKJV)

This is also where we receive understanding from God. He's a master at transforming something bitter into something sweet. He takes our backward steps and moves us forward once again. God now gives Asaph clarity to see the true situation of the wicked:

> "What a slippery path they are on—suddenly God will send them sliding over the edge of the cliff and down to their destruction: an instant end to all their happiness, an eternity of terror."
>
> (Psalm 73:17 LB)

Asaph understands the gravity of life without God. And what a strong picture God has given him. Their happiness won't last forever. They're actually headed for disaster—for eternal separation from God. But just in case Asaph has any lingering pull toward the comparison game, God hammers home the truth again:

> *"Their present life is only a dream! They will awaken to the truth as one awakens from a dream of things that never really were!"*
> (Psalm 73:20 LB)

Asaph is certainly awake now. This is no dream. He fully understands the futility of winning the pride trophy, and he lets it go. In fact, his clarity is so refined now that he actually sympathizes for those who don't know God.

> *"My heart was grieved and my spirit embittered."*
> (Psalm 73:21 NIV)

If we read this verse in the Hebrew language in which Asaph originally wrote this, it says **"I was stabbed in my kidneys."** *Ouch!* What an incredibly powerful image. Further research tells us Asaph is describing having his kidneys being ripped apart by the razor-sharp teeth of a wild beast.

We use the heart to describe our emotions. In the Hebrew culture of Asaph's time, the kidneys were considered the seat of emotions. He admits that all this wrecks him emotionally and physically. But he allowed it to happen, didn't he? He chose to

> God is a master at transforming something bitter into something sweet.

enter the comparison game. He gladly picked up the trophy of pride and allowed it to replace genuine worship.

Don't we all have a choice?

Sometimes we make bad decisions. What began as a quick glance turns into a lingering view. A small bet soon becomes a gambling habit. We choose to take the wrong exit.

The good news is that we have a Redeemer who specializes in complete restoration. And when we continue with Asaph's journal entry, we see that he finds divine redirection.

> "I saw myself so stupid and so ignorant; I must seem like an animal to you, O God. But even so, you love me! You are holding my right hand!"
> (Psalm 73:22-23 LB)

What a God! He continues to love us even when we choose to head the wrong way. He holds our hand and gently guides us in the right direction.

> "You will keep on guiding me all my life with your wisdom and counsel, and afterwards receive me into the glories of heaven! Whom have I in heaven but you? And I desire no one on earth as much as you!"

Asaph has made a complete turnaround. He's engaged in genuine worship. He is praising God and soaking in the incredible love of his Creator. This is the result of true worship. It draws our attention away from ourselves and toward the One who made us for worship. Things aren't perfect for Asaph, but his faith is once again solidified. He has been divinely redirected by his loving Savior.

> "My health fails; my spirits droop, yet God remains! He is the strength of my heart; he is mine forever!"
> (Psalm 73:26 TLB)

God wants to enable us to remain faithful in the *midst* of trials. As Asaph closes his journal, he reminds himself again of what awaits those who refuse to worship God. We can even see him duplicating this from his journal onto a notecard to hang in the dashboard of his chariot as a daily reminder.

> "But those refusing to worship God will perish, for he destroys those serving other gods."
> (Psalm 73:27 LB)

Then Asaph closes his journal entry with a powerful proclamation:

> "But as for me, I get as close to him as I can! I have chosen him, and I will tell everyone about the wonderful ways he rescues me."
> (Psalm 73:28 LB)

But as for me . . .
It's back to choices again.
We all have a decision to make.
What will you specifically do to draw closer to Christ?
Will you consider putting that decision into action right now?

Check out the study section on page 183, then we'll join the two disciples again on their road trip to Emmaus.

Chapter Four
Redirection from a Bad Road Trip

Natasha and her college girlfriends wanted to have a road trip adventure during their spring break. "All five of us were looking forward to getting out of the dorm and enjoying some much-needed fun and relaxation," she says.

"None of us had a specific destination in mind, so we hung a map of the United States on our wall and decided we'd go wherever the dart landed. Kaylee was chosen to toss the dart."

That's how Texas was chosen. But the girls knew they needed to narrow it down. So, they hung a map of Texas on their wall and chose Brittany to throw the dart.

"It landed on Crystal City, Texas," Natasha says. "It wasn't exactly the adventure we were anticipating, but we had fun being together. We discovered Crystal City is the spinach capital of the world. They even have a giant statue of Popeye in front of City Hall."

That was the last time the girls used a dart to decide their spring break whereabouts!

***

Most of us have experienced a disappointing road trip. And that makes it easy to identify with the two disciples we left on the road to Emmaus in chapter two. Let's turn on our navigation system so we can know their precise location.

"Now that same day two of them were going to a village called Emmaus, about seven miles from Jerusalem." (Luke 24:13 NIV)

What same day?

This is Resurrection Day.

"The same day" that Christ rose from the dead, these two guys were on a road trip.

Luke finds Cleopas and his friend leaving Jerusalem. They have heard that a couple of women had found Christ's tomb empty. *Where was His body? Had it been stolen? Moved to a secret location?*

They're wrestling with questions and even arguing among themselves. Again, this is Resurrection Day—the day they should have been expecting. Jesus Himself had told them everything they experienced would actually happen. This would be the day they'd see the reality that He would live once again.

It was the day that victory conquered defeat.

Light had broken through the darkness.

> Jesus is the Son of God; He is God Himself. He is the Messiah.

But because things didn't happen the way they *thought* they should happen, we watch as these men are leaving the city where they were told to wait.

That's right. They had been instructed to wait in Jerusalem. When Jesus tells you to wait—the best thing you can do—is wait.

Cleopas reaches into his backpack and pulls out a few snacks for the road trip. The figs he had picked earlier that day are now a little too soft—and even bruised. He offers one to his friend along with a handful of nuts. They shove the snacks into their mouths and begin arguing between bites.

"They were talking with each other about everything that had happened." (Luke 24:14 NIV)

The original Greek language reveals that these two weren't simply talking—they were actually engaged in a heated argument. Let's eavesdrop on their conversation.

"We should have never placed our faith in Him."

"Well, we were told He was the One!"

"I know. But you can't trust anyone these days."

"You're always cynical."

"At least I'm not gullible."

"You sayin' I'm gullible?"

These two disciples are focused on what they can *see* instead of what Jesus *said*. What do they see? Nothing. They see emptiness. The grave is void of their Savior.

But what did Jesus say? He told them to wait . . . in Jerusalem. And best of all, He said He'd actually rise from the dead after three days. He has kept His promise. But these two guys who were once undaunted in their faith, are no longer focused on Truth—instead they're riveted only by what they can see.

Sierra, from Columbia, S.C., had an unwavering faith in Christ. She attended church regularly and was involved in church activities such as youth group, camp and vacation

Bible school. "I met a girl at camp who said she read the Bible every day. I was so impressed by that. I longed to know God's Word better, so I began reading it on a daily basis as well. I continued that discipline until after college," Sierra says. But after graduating from college and teaching overseas, she found her focus moving from what God had said in His Word to what she could see.

"I discovered a new and dangerous freedom overseas," she says. "I realized I could make my own choices without anyone watching me. I started going the wrong direction. And when I did, my faith quickly weakened."

Sierra let down her guard in the area of purity and enjoyed the attention she received from guys. Though she knew what God had said in the Bible about remaining sexually pure for marriage, she took her eyes off of His Word and became physically involved.

"Though God protected me from STDs and pregnancy, things quickly spiraled downward," she remembers. "None of the men I was with showed me respect or real love. And even though I knew that, I still allowed myself to be used by them. For the next few years I was in a series of bad relationships. As I look back at these events in my life, I'm sickened by them and wish I had kept my eyes on Christ—on what I knew deep in my heart—instead of focusing on only what I wanted at the moment.

"But God was faithful. He continued to reveal Himself to me even though I was definitely living outside of His will. I knew He wanted me back in His arms." Sierra began to see the consequences of her choices and knew her destructive behavior was distancing her from God.

Small Downward Steps

"I remembered a pastor preaching that oftentimes sin doesn't happen with a giant leap—but it's the result of several small acts of disobedience that lead to a lifestyle of rebellion. That's where I was, and I wanted out. I yearned to be back in the arms of my God who loved me inside and out."

Sierra decided to seek God's forgiveness and turn her life around. "When I returned to Him, I felt such a peace—a genuine 'rest' in my soul.

"I eventually met my husband, and God has kept us strong and committed to Him. Yes, there have been hard times—and I've had to do some repair work with people I hurt—but we remain focused on what He says, not on what we can see. I'm learning faith is focusing on what God has said is true even during the times I can't see Him or feel Him. My life isn't perfect, but my life doesn't hurt as it once did. God is definitely my peace."

***

Cleopas and his friend are on the right road, but they're headed the wrong direction. And in their despondency, they continue to argue.

"You believed, didn't you?"

"Yeah, but so did you!"

"I let you talk me into it."

> They had all the right pieces to the puzzle; they just weren't putting it together.

"No, you didn't! You had faith, man. It was your own faith."

"Why'd you let me get my hopes up? He's gone now."

"Hey, you think you're the only one who's feeling this?"

And right in the middle of this heated discussion, Christ appears.

Aren't you glad He joins us in the midst of our struggles and confusion?

"As they talked and discussed these things with each other, Jesus himself came up and walked along with them; but they were kept from recognizing him." (Luke 24:15-16 NIV)

The Wrong Direction Blurs our Vision

Why were they kept from recognizing Him? Christ wasn't wearing a disguise. Could it be they'd become so comfortable with going the wrong direction it was affecting their vision?

Going the wrong direction can do that.

Defeat slaughters the soul.

It prohibits us from seeing the trace of light amid the darkness.

It annihilates hope like an enemy rushing with a lightening-speed sword.

Defeat *is* the enemy.

And his sword glistens with disintegrated dreams.

Jesus Listens

The name Cleopas means *the whole glory of the Father*. Defeat has abducted his identity. Cleopas is no longer living in the glory of his heavenly Father.

But it's into this cancer that the Lion of the Tribe of Judah enters the picture and asks about the argument.

Yes! He intervenes into the very nucleus of our anguish.

"He asked them, 'What are you discussing together as you walk along?' They stood still, their faces downcast." (Luke 24:17 NIV)

They are dumbfounded.
    Bewildered.
        Astonished.
            Flabbergasted.
After an awkward silence, Cleopas finds his voice.

"One of them, named Cleopas, asked him, 'Are you the only one visiting Jerusalem who does not know the things that have happened there in these days?'" (Luke 24:18 NIV)

We can imagine the humorous conversation between them: "Were you born in a barn?"

"As a matter of fact . . ."

"You been living under a rock?"

"For the past three days . . ."

"You don't get out much, do you?"

"Actually, I just got out this morning."

We read in the next few lines of Scripture, that Cleopas recaps the events that recently happened. He tells Jesus of the crucifixion, their dashed dreams and the hope they once had.

And Jesus listens.

He Always Hears

God wants His children to communicate with Him—not simply when they have something good to say—He wants to hear our hearts. God is more than able to handle our rollercoaster emotions. He's strong enough to survive our anger, confusion, arguments and bewilderment.

The Old Testament prophet Habakkuk had a question mark for a brain. The first chapter of his book is filled with questions for God. And these aren't easy questions. Habakkuk launches some perplexing inquiries.

God listened. And answered.

One of Christ's own disciples doubted His Savior's resurrection. Thomas wrestled with questions for an entire week.

Jesus listened. And answered.

When God called Gideon to be the military leader of the Israelites, he doubted, challenged and even tested God . . . twice.

God listened. And answered.

Sarah and Abraham not only questioned God, they actually laughed when He revealed His plan to them about giving birth to a son.

God listened. And answered.

Jeremiah even called the Great I AM a liar.

God listened. And answered.

> When we take our eyes off of *fact* and focus instead on the immediate, it messes with our direction.

It shouldn't surprise us that Jesus also listens to Cleopas and his friend as they detail their hopelessness. Let's continue eavesdropping on the conversation:

> **" 'What things?' he asked.**
> **" 'About Jesus of Nazareth,' they replied.**
> **" 'He was a prophet, powerful in word and deed before God and all the people.' "** (Luke 24:19 NIV)

Not the Whole Truth

It's true; He *was* a prophet. But we know—and they should have known, He was much more than a prophet. Mohammed was a prophet. Jesus is the Son of God; He is God Himself. He is the Messiah.

" 'The chief priests and our rulers handed him over to be sentenced to death, and they crucified him.' " (Luke 24:20 NIV)

"The chief priest condemned him. The crowd killed Him." These two men want to make sure Jesus knows what happened.

OK, we know the rulers *did* kill Him. But let's be clear: They didn't take His life; He gave it!

Jesus Himself said, **"I'm going to Jerusalem. I'll be condemned to death. I will die, but I'll rise again."** (See John 2:18-22.)

Cleopas and his friend are buying into partial truths. That's because defeat keeps us from seeing Jesus clearly, and it's easy to focus on small bits and pieces of truth instead of fixing our eyes on Truth living and incarnate. But truth is absolute, and Jesus affirmed *Himself* as absolute Truth in John 14:6:

"I am the way and the truth and the life. No one comes to the Father except through me." (NIV)

It's dangerous to pick and choose which parts of truth to believe. Doing so always results in bad directions, and we'll find ourselves headed the wrong way.

Let's keep listening:

" 'In addition, some of our women amazed us. They went to the tomb early this morning but didn't find his body.

" 'They came and told us that they had seen a vision of angels, who said he was alive.' " (Luke 24:22-23 NIV)

The women saw a vision of angels? No, they didn't! Read the account. It wasn't a vision of angels.

They.

Saw.

Angels.

There's a big difference between a vision and reality.

This was no dream. Nor was it merely a vision. The women were actually there. With their own eyes, they saw and heard angels.

It's dangerous to buy into partial truth. Doing so can lead to bad doctrine and faulty theology.

" 'Then some of our companions went to the tomb and found it just as the women had said, but they did not see Jesus.' " (Luke 24:24 NIV)

Don't you want to scream: "Open your eyes!"
Here's the problem: They had all the right pieces to the puzzle; they just weren't putting it together. So far this road trip has been anything but good.

Cleopas and his friend had faith, but it was tied to the things they had seen—not to what Jesus had said. And Jesus wants to move them from physical eyes to spiritual eyes.

Adam and Amber from Ashtabula, Ohio learned this lesson the hard way:

"My husband, Adam, and I are planners," Ashley says. "We like to have goals, dates, lists and schedules. This is what keeps us organized and assures our future is under control. At least that's what we *thought*. We discovered that when we commit to God's will, He sometimes has something different in mind—and it doesn't always fit our schedule.

"We've prayed together every night since we were married. Having God's will in our lives is our continuing prayer, but we had no idea that our faith would soon be tested.

"My husband was finally out of school, and we had both worked several part-time jobs that added up to fulltime income that we had saved so we could start planning for our first child. After waiting nine years to conceive, we finally had a sweet, healthy baby boy. The plan was for me to go back to work, my mother-in-law would babysit fulltime, and we'd have a balanced happy future for our family.

"God had a different plan."

After Jaxson was born, Adam's job dwindled in hours, and he ended up only racking up 10 hours of work per week. Amber was on maternity leave and was praying God would allow her to be a stay-at-home mom. Their secure future was now in jeopardy with little finances to lean on.

"Adam got up early one morning with Jaxson and prayed while rocking him back to sleep. He asked God to provide him with jobs to keep our bills paid. At 8 a.m., he received a call for a house remodel, and by 8:30 a.m., he landed a job for another remodel. By 9 a.m., he had a third offer. We were praising God!"

Though Adam and Amber were grateful for back-to-back side-jobs, they knew they needed more if she was going to get to stay home with the baby after maternity leave. "Adam was longing for a steady career with benefits. Part-time handyman jobs continued to flow for him, and while they knew God was providing for them, Adam continued to apply for fulltime positions.

"We have always been tithers and simply believe that tithing is an act of obedience and a great way to show our love for God. But why couldn't we find a fulltime job? We felt defeated," Amber says. "And the defeat was drowning our praise to God for His daily provision.

"Sure, we knew what God proclaimed in His Word: **"I was young and now I am old, yet I have never seen the righteous forsaken or their children begging bread"** (Psalm 27:25 NIV). And we knew there would eventually be an end to our drought . . . but when? It's as though we had forgotten how to see through our spiritual eyes. We were only looking at our circumstances through our immediate physical eyes."

Testing

Adam and Amber experienced a rollercoaster of emotions—spiritually and mentally. Nine months passed, and there was still no hint of any fulltime jobs.

"The feeling of defeat was a daily burden," Amber says. "I was eventually tested on something I never thought was a struggle: giving. I had always seen myself as a cheerful giver. It had been easy for me to give—as long as life was flowing with milk and honey," she says. "But when times were tough financially, my open hands started to draw back."

Adam sensed God telling him to make a table and give it away. "He has always been a willing servant," Amber says. "But I was hesitant to this idea. I chose to believe that God had given us the material to construct this table in order for us to sell it and receive some needed income."

As Amber continued her daily Bible study the next morning, she discovered the subject was on giving. She was immediately convicted to have a giver's heart and to be used by God to help someone else in need.

"We gave the table away," she says. "It felt good, but I admit there was pain in this offering. And my test wasn't done!"

Amber felt God's nudge to give away a baby item she had found at a great price for Jaxson. "I tried ignoring the Holy Spirit; after all, I had purchased this item for *my* child. Though my head wanted one thing, my heart was leading me to do the *right* thing. I gave this sweet baby item to a missionary friend. And though I know she was appreciative, I again experienced pain in my offering.

"A couple of months later, I received a big surprise. That same gift—identical to the one I had purchased—was given to me as a Christmas gift! God cared. I know it was a material thing that I didn't *have* to have, but God saw this mother's heart and cared about my desires for my baby."

More Testing

Amber thought her testing was finished but soon learned God would continue to ask more. "Each time I was tested, I hesitated with a worldly heart. My husband was again nudged by the Holy Spirit to give. This time, it was a large cut of our income tax return. When he asked for my input, I cried like a baby. But after the tears I agreed we needed to obey God in everything."

Eleven months later, with a baby in tow, Amber remembers each day as hard as the previous. "We felt the heaviness of defeat. We were planners; this wasn't supposed to happen. Though we knew God's promises, we were only focused on what we could *see*. And what we were seeing . . . was nothing.

Adam and Amber continued to follow God's direction in their lives. "We soaked ourselves with every Sunday school lesson, every sermon and Bible study we could to keep ourselves drowning in our self-pity," she says. "I prayed often for the Lord to speak to Adam. I knew he was depressed. We were both tired of not hearing from God and wondering when things would change.

"One morning Adam woke up from a dream. He believed it was from God, and it was a dream of provision and hope."

In the dream, God has asked him to choose any of six doors to a barn and open it. After Adam had opened the door he chose, God opened all of the doors to the barn. He saw the entire barn filled to the top with hay.

"We knew exactly what God was telling us," Amber says. "He was going to fill our storehouses. He would provide—no matter the avenue He'd take us. That was such a day of hope for us!"

A Large Purchase

Twelve months later, Adam and Amber received a phone call from a friend. She gave them the name of a woman who was looking for someone with Adam's skills. "This job was something he had already applied for and hadn't received an interview, but he quickly re-applied," Amber says.

"Meanwhile, we needed to purchase a truck for Adam's construction business on the side. The vehicle we had was worn out. And it was really too small for Jaxson's car seat. My knees were in the dashboard anytime I rode passenger, and it just wasn't safe. We definitely needed this newer and larger truck and felt God prompting us to make the purchase. It was scary to move forward in faith—without seeing any money coming in—but we obeyed and bought it."

A few days later, Adam landed the fulltime position with benefits that allowed flexibility for his extra side-jobs for more income. "This road was long and hard for us," Amber admits. "We were impatient, angry at times, defeated and even depressed. But we learned that we can't focus on what we can *see;* we have to stay riveted on what God has *said*. And His direction is always right."

***

Cleopas and his friend had the clues, but they didn't see Him. They were defeated. They were discouraged. They were on the right road—but they were going the wrong direction—and this was causing them to miss the celebration happening with the disciples in Jerusalem. When we take our eyes off of *fact* and focus instead on the immediate, it messes with our direction. Actually, it has been known to completely break our spiritual compass.

Our two friends are walking with labored steps. Let's allow them to rest for a bit. We'll join them later. After you've finished the study section on page 184, let's chat about a road all of us will walk at least once in our lives.

Chapter Five
Redirection from Hopelessness

Names are important.

Your name is the first thing that people usually ask of you, what you'll be asked the most, and it's how you'll be known for the rest of your life.

Even Romeo and Juliet were into the name game. You may recall Shakespeare's lyrical tale of their doomed love. When these two members of warring families collided with affection, Juliet asked, "What's in a name? That which we call a rose by any other name would smell as sweet." Despite her romantic overtures, they weren't able to rise above Montague or Capulet.

Yes, names matter.

Here's the story of *my* name. (Well, it's the story my older brother told me. And, because Mom and Dad never corrected him, I believe it.)

My name is Billy Andrew Huddleston. My family is Appalachian, so Billy is on my birth certificate. Not William. Not Bill. It's Billy. I do, however, have people who wish to make me a William or Bill. One man even said going by Billy makes me sound 7 years old.

It's. My. Name.

Billy Andrew Huddleston.

When I was born, my parents wanted to name me after a double cousin (he was related to both mom and dad), Billy Herald, who lost his life at an early age in a tragic automobile accident. They also wanted to name me after my great grandfather Drew. Would it be Billy Drew? Drew Billy? Billy Drew?

Having tried every combination, going around and round, they were unable to decide. So, they named me Billy *and* Drew: Billy Andrew Huddleston.

***

Many names have a story. See if you can match the following names with the correct celebrity. Go ahead and draw a line from the names in the column on the left to the name you think it matches in the column on the right.

Mark Sinclair	Elton John
Margaret Mary Emily Anne Hyra	Demi Moore
Peter Gene Hernandez	Vin Diesel
Reginald Kenneth Dwight	Meg Ryan
Demetria Gene Guynes	Bruno Mars

Here are the explanations behind those names and to whom they belong. Margaret Mary Emily Anne Hyra = Meg Ryan. Meg took her grandmother's maiden name when she became a professional actress.

Mark Sinclair = Vin Diesel. He shortened his mom's maiden name Vincent and attached it to his nickname "Diesel" given to him by friends who said he always had an ample supply of energy.

Peter Gene Hernandez = Bruno Mars. His dad has been calling him Bruno since the musician was 2 years old. Bruno attached the word Mars as his last name because he thought it sounded bigger than life.

Demetria Gene Guynes = Demi Moore. She wanted a shorter name for show business, so she simply shortened her first name, and her last name is from her first marriage to singer Freddy Moore.

> Don't give your situation today the naming rights for your tomorrow.

Reginald Kenneth Dwight = Elton John. When he began his public music career, he took the first name of two blues legends: Elton Dean was a saxophonist, and Long John Baldry was a singer.

Names in the Bible

Many names in Scripture have a specific meaning. Jacob means "Heel grabber" (see chapter nine). He was named this because when he was born, his hand was on the heel of his twin brother, Esau. By the way, Esau means "Hairy." He was born with thick red hair.

Saul stands for "inquired of God." Ruth denotes companion and friend. Gideon means destroyer. Phoebe signifies radiant, pure. Timothy indicates honor given to God. And Matthew means gift of God. By the way, Walter isn't mentioned in the Bible, but in case you're wondering, it means "ruler of the army." Seems as though the Old

Testament had several of those, but they were called David, Jephthah, Gideon, Saul and other names. But no Walters.

There are two names in the Bible that seem to be incredibly significant, and they stand in stark contrast to one another: Immanuel and Ichabod.

Sad Story

Before we dive inside Ichabod's story, we need the prequel, and we get it through Eli's story (1 Samuel 4). He was a devout and godly man. He served as the High Priest in Shiloh and as Israel's judge for 40 years. By the time we catch up with him in 1 Samuel 4, he's 90 years old. He's lived a full life of service to God and his people.

Eli's sons Hophni and Phinehas were a different story. The Bible paints them as irreverent, ungodly, careless, and irreligious. They were scoundrels and scandalous. Here's the biblical description:

"Now the sons of Eli were corrupt; they did not know the LORD." (1 Samuel 2:12 NKJV)

> God often works quietly behind the scenes.

It's interesting that such a good man would have such bad sons. Part of the problem was that Eli failed to take his responsibilities as a father seriously. He could have easily stepped in and corrected them, but he didn't. (For more insight, check out 1 Samuel 2:22-25.)

Being weak and indulgent as a father overshadowed Eli's faithful service to God and the people. This would ultimately be the ruin of Eli and his two sons. The tragic consequence is recorded in 1 Samuel 4.

Here's the scene: Israel was engaged in battle with the Philistines.

Again.

The Philistines were notorious for harassing God's people. And they lost this specific battle big time. In fact, it was a major wipeout with more than 4,000 Israelites killed.

Whenever God directed the battle, it ended in victory. But when the Israelites failed to let Him lead, they always lost. This was a vicious cycle repeating itself again and again and yes . . . *again*.

Wouldn't you think the Israelites would catch on?

When they should have been repenting, they were scratching their heads instead.

How could this happen? Where could we have gone wrong? Why would God allow it? They schemed and eventually came up with a plan. They decided to take the Ark of the Covenant with them to the battlefield.

This is not a plan of strategy; it's a plan filled with arrogance. They think they can force God's hand to give them victory by hauling the Ark around like a good luck charm. God is not mocked, nor will He be controlled.

Sometimes we find ourselves in the same situation. When life is going well, we continue forward with our own plans. But when things go wrong? *That's* when we look to Him. Elizabeth recalls just such a time:

It was the middle of my sophomore year in college, and things were going great. I had several friends and was excelling academically. I was—and still am—a people-person and enjoyed being involved in campus life and moving forward with my own plans.

But in the midst of my good life, I suddenly went into a deep depression. I realize many people believe Christians shouldn't struggle with depression, but emotional abuse during my teen years—paired with a chemical imbalance—created the perfect storm. I had battled depression before college but the counseling I had sought, paired with help from my physician, helped me experience a healthy emotional state. But in the middle of my sophomore year, I hit bottom.

I found little purpose in life, began withdrawing from close relationships and spent most of my time in bed or driving around listening to sad music.

The pain I was feeling became unbearable, and I simply found no joy or purpose in life. It seemed as though I was trying to breathe through tar. I felt like a burden to those around me and thought God had walked away. So I decided to take my own life.

I headed into my bedroom and washed down a bottle of Xanax with a bottle of NyQuil, hoping I'd drift away from my problems, forever. After sleeping for a very long time, to my surprise, I woke up.

I decided if God wanted to keep me around, I'd do things His way. I sought help, and during the treatment for my depression, I devoted time to spend with Jesus. Days spent in prayer and studying Scripture helped give me the courage, strength and discipline to construct my time in ways that were lifegiving.

I continued treatment, but this time with a new attitude and new faith in how God could use me and how He could give wisdom to those helping me. I was able to clearly see what a mess I was and recognized my need of His guidance.

But more than anything, I realized He *wanted* to give me His love and grace, and that made all the difference.

I've learned the lesson of not simply seeking Him first when things are going badly, but to diligently pursue Him every single day.

Meanwhile...

When the Israelites arrived at the Temple in Shiloh, Hophni and Phinehas were there with the Ark. They entered the battle and were dealt a tremendous defeat: 30,000 soldiers were killed—including Hophni and Phinehas.

The Philistines not only annihilated a mammoth loss of lives, but they also captured the Ark of God. So the symbol of God's Presence among His people was now absent. By this time, Eli was 98 years old and blind. He was sitting in a chair by the side of the road waiting for a runner to bring him news of the battle. When he heard what had happened, he fell from his chair, broke his neck and died.

But that's not the end of the story.

The wife of Phinehas was pregnant (see 1 Samuel 4:19), and her due date was just around the corner. When she heard the news of the battle and the deaths of her husband, her brother-in-law and Eli—as well as the news about the Ark—she went into premature labor and gave birth to a baby boy. Her labor was horrific, and she died. But with her last few breaths, she named her baby boy Ichabod. The meaning? *The glory of God has departed; no glory.*

"Then she named the child Ichabod, saying, "The glory has departed from Israel!" because the ark of God had been captured and because of her father-in-law and her husband." 1 Samuel 4:21 (NKJV)

No Glory

Ichabod.

The glory of God has departed.

This is what he will be known as the rest of his life. This became his identity. Glory-less. Hope-less. He was branded by his name.

Let's recap what we have so far, because we have a lot of people on the wrong road traveling the wrong direction.

- The Israelites (God's chosen people) have taken the wrong exit. They pulled off the right road of serving God and completely neglected Him to take an exit they thought was a shortcut. In doing so, they've now hit a dead-end with 34,000 thousand deaths and the loss of the Ark—God's symbol of His presence.

- Eli was on the right road, but he was headed the wrong direction. He loved God and served Him wholeheartedly. But he was a lousy parent with no discipline or follow-through. He, too, hit a dead-end and lost his sons and his own life.

- Hophni and Phinehas were never on the right road and had no intention of turning around. Their demise was their unwillingness to repent of their evil actions.

- The wife of Phineas may have been on the right road, but she certainly created her own roadblock by naming her son "The Glory of God Has Departed."

- Ichabod—"No Glory"—was set in motion toward the wrong direction as soon as he was born simply because he was branded with a hopeless name that intertwined with his lifestyle.

We needed the above list of characters to set the scene for Ichabod. But at this point, he's the only one alive among the cast, so let's focus on him now.

Still No Glory?

Because Phinehas had died in battle, his wife had "naming rights" of their newborn son. She obviously allowed her grief and defeat to overshadow her choice of a name. By doing this, she allowed her present circumstances to define her son, "The Glory of God Has Departed," and his middle name was "No Glory."

This is a battle we, too, often fight.

Let's resolve to rise above this temptation.

Don't give your situation today the naming rights for your tomorrow. Life isn't always easy nor fun. But God is always good. It's easy for us to become trapped in our present situation—to become stuck in front of a roadblock that we forget about Hope incarnate.

When your every step is labored, and you can't even see an exit off the road on which you're imprisoned, know that God hasn't left you on the side of the road.

> When it seems that all hope is gone—be assured—God is at work!

The sun will shine again.

This is temporary.

Don't allow you present circumstance to have naming rights for your tomorrow. Let God redirect your present into the tomorrow He has in store for you.

God often works quietly behind the scenes—as He did in Sheron's story:

I feel as though I've experienced my share of heartache. A fire totally destroyed my home, I lost my 12-year-old son to leukemia, and a 300-pound sign fell 16 feet from the side of a building and left my husband with many injuries including total memory loss.

But none of those things could have prepared me for the shock of when my husband of 32 years asked me for a divorce. I would have never imagined that would be something we'd go through. But, that's where we were.

I was dumbfounded, but I continued to try and be the "hands of Jesus" to him. I prepared a nice dinner for him every night, made sure his clothes were clean and even helped him pick out furniture for his new apartment.

I prayed and lived inside the Psalms. But, nothing changed. How could 32 years of marriage be gone just like that? For three months I moved in a state of fog. I didn't realize that God was at work behind the scenes.

After those three months, while I was at work (praying the prayer that I had been praying: "Please God, help him come to his senses"), I received a call from my estranged husband. He wanted to meet during my lunch hour to talk.

I'll never forget our conversation in the family room that day. He told me he wanted to come back home, and he asked if we could remarry. He told me the whole time I was helping him, God was dealing with him. He used these words, "I've come to my senses." That had been my exact prayer.

There were so many times I knew God was bringing me through. I didn't know how or when, but I never let go of Him. After my husband moved out, there were times I didn't want to go on; I really wanted to die.

But God's sweet Spirit consistently ministered to me during those days. He was so near there were times I felt as though I could physically touch Him. I asked God not only to be my Father, but to be my companion, my husband.

God has done such a work in our lives and in our relationship that we have never been closer than we are now. God is faithful!

***

We often can't see God working quietly behind the scenes. And during those times, it's easy to let our circumstances hi-jack us from the right road. That's the spirit of Ichabod—and many times it seems to reign supreme.

But it doesn't have to.

There is another name.

Happy Endings Aren't Just in Fairy Tales

When it seems that all hope is gone—be assured—God is at work! The thing about the Ichabod spirit is that it seems to be the overarching plight of mankind. No matter what they do they'll never be who they were intended to be. Everything seems hopeless. But, God is at work. Check out this promise from Isaiah 7:14:

"Therefore, the Lord Himself will give you a sign: Behold, the virgin shall conceive and bear a Son, and shall call His name Immanuel." (NKJV)

A promise is only as good as the one who makes it. There have been many promises made and broken. But, when God makes a promise, you can take it to the bank!

While the Ichabod spirit is seemingly in control, God is moving behind the scenes. And, what He is about to do will be the deathblow to hopelessness.

Let's read the fulfillment of this promise. It's found in Matthew 1:18-25:

"Now the birth of Jesus Christ was as follows: After His mother Mary was betrothed to Joseph, before they came together, she was found with child of the Holy Spirit. Then Joseph her husband, being a just man, and not wanting to make her a public example, was minded to put her away secretly. But while he thought about these things, behold, an angel of the Lord appeared to him in a dream, saying, 'Joseph, son of David, do not be afraid to take to you Mary your wife, for that which is conceived in her is of the Holy Spirit. And she will bring forth a Son, and you shall call His name JESUS, for He will save His people from their sins.'

"So all this was done that it might be fulfilled which was spoken by the Lord through the prophet, saying: 'Behold, the virgin shall be with child, and bear a Son, and they shall call His name Immanuel,' which is translated, 'God with us.' " (NKJV)

God looked across time and saw us in our hopeless condition. His heart was so moved that He sent His Son from the perfection of heaven to a fallen world in order to crush hopelessness. This changes everything!

Back to Ichabod

What happened to Ichabod? He's only mentioned one other time in the Bible—10 chapters later—and it's only in reference to his nephew, Ahijah, who's a high priest. Maybe Ichabod continued with the family ministry as well. We don't know. Did he ever climb out of his derogatory name?

We like to root for the underdog, and we hope Ichabod rose above his negative circumstances. We want to believe he was used by God and made a positive difference in Israel. But we don't have any information.

Wouldn't it be great if he broke the cycle?

Wouldn't it be great if *we* broke the cycle?

Are you missing the glory of God in your life? God has a plan for you; it's to divinely redirect you. He wants to turn you around and let you see His glory. He wants you to *experience* His glory.

"And we all, who with unveiled faces contemplate the Lord's glory, are being transformed into his image with ever-increasing glory, which comes from the Lord, who is the Spirit." (1 Corinthians 3:18 NIV)

> Experiencing His glory involves transformation.
> Worship.
> Obedience.
> And a divine turnaround.

But like Ichabod, we have a choice. We can let our circumstances determine our lives, or we can use our lives—empowered by God—to change our circumstances. We can choose to let His glory transform us from the inside out.

Like Ichabod, others will often try to label us. We get to choose what to do with those labels. Will we own them or reject them? If you've accepted the name of Ichabod, it's time to release it.

There is another name.

Immanuel.

God is with us.

The Spirit of Immanuel is greater than the spirit of Ichabod.

And this changes everything.

After you've finished the study section on page 185, let's look at a road on which many of us find ourselves.

Chapter Six
Redirection from Worthlessness

He had a funny name: Mephibosheth
(Muh-FIB-O-sheth).
But unfortunately, he wasn't known by his name.
He was known by his handicap:
He was crippled in both feet. His label had defined him.
Maybe you know what it's like to be known by a label:
- the divorced one
- the alcoholic
- the one who had an abortion
- the black sheep
- the one who can't hold down a job

Stan once wore the label of Worthless.

I grew up in a Christian home near Indianapolis, and I've always struggled with my weight. My family was extremely involved in a great church, and I accepted Christ as my Savior when I was just 5 years old. I know some people don't think that a child can understand the process of salvation, but I definitely knew what I was doing when I asked Christ to come into my heart and forgive my sins. Even as a little boy, I knew I needed a Savior.

Even though I grew in my faith and loved the involvement I had in church, I felt insecure because of my weight. But I continued to trust God, and I joined the quiz team. I quickly rose to the top and absolutely loved studying and memorizing the Bible. God continued to become more real and more personal to me each day—even though my weight was still a major struggle for me.

When I was 16, God impressed on me that He was calling me into fulltime ministry—specifically missionary service. And even *more* specific—He was calling me to linguistics. I had heard stories of missionaries who would live with a tribe and simply listen to their language that was unknown to the rest of the world. During the years spent with the tribe, they'd learn the language, write it down, teach the people how to read it and eventually write the New Testament into their language.

God's Calling

I was genuinely drawn to this calling. But when I shared this with my parents, my dad expressed his disappointment. "You'll never amount to anything in this field. Don't throw your life away with this." And although Mom wasn't as vocal, she never encouraged me.

This lack of support from my dad—along with the insecurity with my weight—made me feel worthless. My relationship with God, however, was extremely strong and I didn't waiver. I applied to a university that offered a linguistics program and graduated excited about all I'd learned. I then entered a graduate program specializing in African languages. I loved the process of learning how to create a dictionary from a language that had never been written, and how to discern vowels and consonants from clicks, guttural throat sounds and unfamiliar words. It truly fascinated me, and I began to realize that God had gifted me in this specialized area of ministry.

But in college and even through my graduate work, I continued to wear the label of Worthless because of my dad's insistence on this undesirable career and my weight. After my father passed away, I carried the label onto the mission field.

I joined Wycliff Bible translators, and though I continued to battle feelings of insecurity, God enabled me to decipher languages and to live among several different tribes of pygmies deep in the bush of Cameroon, Africa. As I loved the people—and as I shared the good news of God's love for them—I began to see His tremendous faithfulness on my calling and to see myself through His eyes and not my own.

God has allowed me to teach specialized deciphering methods to other linguists and is helping me walk away from that label of Worthless. It still rears its ugly head once in a while, but I'm now striving to live with His label—*Chosen*—and what a difference it's making in my life. He is redirecting my self-image.

***

Mephibosheth Was Crippled

It was hard to remember the day when he *wasn't* wearing a label. He was a man who had been forced onto the wrong exit ramp.

The interesting thing about labels is that God doesn't see them. And He never uses them. From God's view, you are never seen as a label. You are seen as His special, chosen one. He calls you by your name—not a label. (Need proof? See Isaiah 43, 44, 45.)

Back to Mephibosheth. His father was Jonathan—King David's best friend. Jonathan was the son of King Saul. Long before David became king of Israel, he and Jonathan made a covenant.

A covenant is much more than a promise; it's a holy oath. It doesn't depend on the reaction of the other person. Here's the ultimate example: God made a covenant with us. He sent His Son, Jesus, to die on a cross for our sins. Whether or not we accept the covenant, God still holds His end. Jesus still died for your sins. Choosing to accept that is up to you, but it doesn't change God's covenant.

> Some of us have become comfortable living in a way that God never intended for us.

David and Jonathan's covenant was that each would look after the family of the other in the event one should die. Let's push the fast-forward button. Years have passed. King Saul and his son Jonathan have been killed in battle. David has ascended the throne. God has blessed him and grown his kingdom.

One day David remembers the covenant he made with Jonathan and wants to show kindness—or take care of—any of Jonathan's family members who may still be living.

Let's look at the Scripture:

"The king then asked him, "Is anyone left from Saul's family? If so, I want to fulfill a sacred vow by being kind to him."

"Yes," Ziba replied, "Jonathan's lame son is still alive." (2 Samuel 9:3 LB)

Did you notice that Scripture doesn't even mention the name of Jonathan's son? He's known only by his handicap.

In many versions of the Bible, he's bracketed into Scripture.

He's merely a parenthesis. Take a look:

"**(Jonathan son of Saul had a son who was lame in both feet. He was five years old when the news about Saul and Jonathan came from Jezreel.**

"**His nurse picked him up and fled, but as she hurried to leave, he fell and became disabled. His name was Mephibosheth).**" (2 Samuel 4:4 NIV)

It's Not Fair

Do you ever feel as though you're simply a parenthetical expression? Not worth much? Just bracketed into existence?

Life had not been fair to Mephibosheth.

It had started out great!

Because he was royalty, he enjoyed the many privileges of living with Grandpa King Saul and Dad—Prince Jonathan. Back then Mephibosheth even had a royal name: Mirab Baal.

It meant "Opponent of Baal."

Baal was a false, pagan god.

A vile idol.

So "Opponent of Baal" was a strong name that carried warrior qualities.

But now this boy's name was different.

Mephibosheth meant "Son of Shame."

His name was changed all because of what happened that one day many years ago. When he was a little boy—

probably 6 years old—a man, bruised and exhausted from battle, ran through the palace gates and screamed, "King Saul and his sons are dead!"

Back then, Mephibosheth didn't understand it all, but a cold chill ran through his little body, and suddenly the palace became a place of panic. Wives wept; servants were blanched with fear.

Mephibosheth remembered how his nurse came running up to him with a few things in her hand and yelled, "Run Mirab Baal—your life depends on it!"

He didn't understand, but he ran with her as hard as he could.

But his 6-year-old legs could only go so fast and so far.

Knowing the urgency, his nurse picked him up—and with Mirab Baal in her arms, she ran for their lives. But in the rocky, winding hills, she slipped and dropped him.

Mephibosheth crashed on his feet, and severe pain overtook him.

Both of his feet were broken.

But they couldn't think about seeking help now.

Survival was the issue.

She picked him up and continued to carry him. His bones never mended correctly. He would never walk again.

Imagine his pain inside as he watched the other boys and girls his age running and jumping and playing—and he knew that he would never be a part of that.

Mephibosheth would forever be dependent on others just to transport him from place to place. And as he reflected on his misfortune, one wonders if he thought to himself again and again,

Why me? This wasn't my fault!

Headed in the Wrong Direction

Maybe you can relate. Have you experienced something that hasn't been your fault?

"My life wasn't supposed to be like this."

"My spouse wasn't supposed to reject me."

"She wasn't supposed to die this young."

"I wasn't supposed to be raising my grandkids."

"I shouldn't have lost my job."

Remember Stan? Though he had released his label of Worthless and was striving to accept himself through God's eyes, he experienced several trials living in the bush with pygmy tribes.

I was living in a little home deep in the jungle. This was area was inhabited by pygmy tree-hunters. They used bows and arrows to shoot things from trees to eat (birds, monkeys, etc.) I had to leave their village for a couple of weeks, and unfortunately communication between the villagers and me was still in the beginning stages. I was working diligently to understand them, decipher their language and begin writing it down for them.

During my short absence, the owner of the land my house was on misunderstood my absence. He thought I was trying to skip paying him rent. He violently killed my dog, Rocky, and strategically placed the carcass on the roof of my home so I couldn't help but see it when I returned.

My heart broke. Because I'm single, I counted on that little dog as my constant buddy. He had provided much comfort to me in the heart of a jungle with no modern conveniences. This exacerbated my loneliness. I was tempted to question God. *Why did this happen? It wasn't my fault. Yet I'm the one who is deeply grieved.*

I mourned a long time for Rocky. I missed him greatly. But I continued to pray for the tribesmen and worked with their language. Eventually—with God's help—I was able to forgive.

***

An Innocent Victim

It wasn't Mephibosheth's fault that he was handicapped. Because his nurse took the wrong exit, he'd been heading in the wrong direction ever since.

He needed a turn-around.

Well, he *did* make a turn, but it still wasn't in the right direction.

For many years he lived in secrecy, being cared for by others in Lo Debar. Lo Debar was a city east of the Jordan River. The whole area is a barren wasteland. The literal meaning of Lo Debar is "the place of no bread." You have to be desperate to be living in "the place of no bread."

Mephibosheth was hiding out in a desolate place.

He also lived with the constant fear for his own life, because David was getting stronger as king. Mephibosheth's family was getting weaker and dying off. Would he be next?

You see, the custom in those times was that when a new king took the throne, he killed the remaining members of the previous king's family so there wouldn't be any chance of a take-over.

Mephibosheth knew that any day he could receive a knock on the door and be taken away to be executed or tortured or both. So he had to live the rest of his life without his father and with a severe disability. Whenever he's mentioned in the Bible from then on—his disability is also mentioned. He is known by a label.

Comfortable on the Wrong Road

How many nights did he wonder how long it would be before the soldiers would come for him?

How many days did he look down that dirt road and wonder if today would be the day they'd take him away?

As the years came and went, he probably began to feel more comfortable living in Lo Debar.

> The King pursues you.

Unfortunately, some of us have become comfortable living in a way that God never intended for us; we've become used to going the wrong direction . . . settling into a lifestyle that's less than His best for us.

But here's the truth: You are a child of the King!

You were never meant to live in Lo Debar.

You were meant to live in the palace!

Here we have Mephibosheth—crippled and broken—living in despair with no hope. He has no idea there's a king in Jerusalem who loves him and is searching for him.

Just like your King!

We have the same basic problem Mephibosheth had:

He was crippled, and so are we.

He had learned to exist going in the wrong direction.

But the good news is that, like Mephibosheth, we are sought by the King. He pursues you. He wants you.

We can see Mephibosheth sitting outside his humble house one morning and viewing the soldiers coming down the dirt road. He'd seen this in his mind a million times before and every time he had imagined it, it was disaster.

When the soldiers reached his home, they told Mephibosheth that the king wanted to talk with him. They took Mephibosheth into custody and began the journey back to the palace.

As they traveled, we imagine that Mephibosheth began preparing himself for his death. *How will it happen? Will I be executed? Beaten? How will this be played out? How long will I suffer before my last breath?*

Divine Redirection

When they arrived at the palace, Mephibosheth was ushered into the presence of the king.

David said, "Mephibosheth!"

He called him by his name—not by a label.

Let's keep reading as 2 Samuel 9:1 unfolds itself.

" **'Don't be afraid,' David said to him. 'I will restore to you all the land that belonged to your grandfather Saul, and you will always eat at my table.' "** (NLT)

He would never have to be afraid again. He would be under the king's protection. David would restore to him all the land of his grandfather, Saul. Best of all, he would eat at David's table regularly with all of his family.

David didn't simply receive Mephibosheth as a friend, he accepted him as his son—one who could enjoy the constant companionship of the king and eat at his table.

How did Mephibosheth respond?

"Mephibosheth bowed down and said, 'Who is your servant, that you should show such kindness to a dead

dog like me?' "

This shows how low his self-esteem was. Spending years headed in the wrong direction can do that. In biblical times, a dog was nothing. It was equivalent to trash. Mephibosheth doesn't even feel worthy of being compared to a living dog.

He calls himself a dead dog. Useless garbage.

Have you ever felt that low?

There's a King who's reaching out to you. Jesus Christ, the King of kings, desires to redirect your life. And guess where He's leading you?

Right inside the palace. Directly into His presence.

Mephibosheth expected the king's wrath; instead, he got the king's unconditional love and acceptance. He was still lame—but, he was no longer an orphan, no longer living in fear—for now, he was sitting at the king's table, as one of his own sons.

That's divine redirection.

Can You Relate?

Maybe you, too, long for acceptance. Perhaps you hunger for someone to see past your handicap—whether emotional or physical— and know your heart.

You've been disappointed by some of life's tragedies:

- Serious illness has touched you or someone you love.
- Fear has gripped you, and you're overwhelmed by suffering, finances, the future, ridicule, etc.
- You've been rejected by someone you love.

***

When Stan was 30 years old, his mom remarried a man she met on a missions trip. He was extremely active in their church and even served on the church board. But things weren't as they seemed.

I returned home for furlough and stayed in a little house my mom owned that was close to where she and my new stepdad lived. I wasn't there long before the abuse began. He verbally berated me: "You're a loser. You don't have a real job. You have to raise support and depend on the goodness of others to do what you're doing."

That old label of Worthless tried to attach itself to me again. This man was evil. He played the Christian game at church, but when we were at home, he turned into a violent, deranged monster. He was 6' 4" and he was a body-builder, and he hurled insult after insult at me for being overweight.

"You've ruined God's temple," he said. "You're fat. You're worthless." I knew that lashing back at him wouldn't do any good, and God gave me the strength to remain calm.

There were several times he held my head in the toilet until I repeated his favorite phrase: "I'm no good."

I'm 5' 4" so I couldn't fight him. Remember, this guy was a body-builder. He was rock-solid. And I knew if I *did* try to stand up for myself, he'd abuse my mom. So, I took it.

My birth father—though a Christian—had rejected my call to follow God to the mission field and was ashamed that I didn't have a normal job. Now my stepfather had rejected me and was enjoying his ability to abuse me. I often silently asked, "Why me?"

***

You, Too?

Maybe . . . just like Mephibosheth . . . and like Stan . . . you're also asking *Why me?*

Your support systems are broken.

Your spiritual life is out of joint.

Perhaps you wonder if God has become your enemy. You fear Him. And so, in your helplessness, you're running from Him, fleeing from His presence.

But right now, I hope you hear His call to you: **"Come before My throne."**

You expect the worst: judgment, wrath.

But when you come to Him, you'll be totally surprised by His grace. All the wrath of God for your sin falls upon Christ, and to YOU, God says, "Come! Eat at my table. You are Mine! You are a child of the King of kings!"

He's offering you a place at His own table—every single night!

That's intimacy.

That's divine redirection.

That's grace.

> When you come to Him, you'll be totally surprised by His grace.

Restoration

Stan experienced a lot of abuse from his stepdad, but he continued to pray for him. After his year furlough was over, Stan returned to his work in Africa.

While I was away from home, my stepfather didn't want me calling Mom, so I didn't get to talk with her often. But after a few years, she got word to me that he was battling pancreatic cancer and had been placed in home hospice.

I got permission from Wycliff to return home, and God gave me the grace to care for him. I was hoping for restoration. I longed for him to seek forgiveness and for things to be peaceful between us. That never happened.

Things he said and did to me have had a devastating effect on my life. I also still deal with the lack of emotional support from my birth dad. Both men made poor choices that severely hurt me.

But God is close. And He's teaching me that I'm chosen. He's helping me become more secure in the fact that HE wants to give me what my birth father and my stepfather never did. I'll be honest: It's a slow process. But I know my heavenly Father is committed to making me whole.

***

Has life dealt you some devastating blows? Your heavenly Father wants to bring total restoration. It may not come immediately, but He is faithful to complete everything He starts (see Philippians 1:6 for proof).

He has extended your personal invitation to sit at the table with Him. Are you sitting at the table of the King?

Are you enjoying this kind of intimacy with Him?

If not, what's standing in the way?

    Crippled feet?
        Handicapped heart?
            Damaged emotions?
                Cumbersome baggage?

Give it up.
Get His grace.

Come . . . and sit at His table.
Enjoy genuine intimacy with Him.
YOU are a child of the King.

Please make time to complete the study section on page 186. Then we'll discover how someone received victory after being handed a death sentence.

Chapter Seven
Redirection from a Death Sentence

He was God-blessed, God-directed and God-used—as well as great and admirable. In fact, any positive adjective would be fitting to describe him: amazing, incredible, terrific, gifted, astonishing, fabulous, remarkable, outstanding . . . the list could go on and on.

God had given him tremendous victory over neighboring armies. And through him, God had led the Syrian army to become the strongest battalion of its time. In fact, Syria itself was the most dominant region in the Western part of Asia.

His name was Naaman, and he was the leader of the Syrian army. He was a five-star general. Today he could easily be a governor or a state senator. He was a great leader and possessed shining brilliance and people skills.

King Ben-Hadad (ruler of Syria) greatly admired his right-hand man, Naaman and had the utmost confidence in this general.

But despite all these wonderful accolades regarding Naaman, five words reduce it all to nothing. Take a look at the last five words in 1 Kings 5:1 from the Living Bible:

"The king of Syria had high admiration for Naaman, the commander-in-chief of his army, for he had led his

troops to many glorious victories. So he was a great hero, but he was a leper."

"But he was a leper" reduces everything he has accomplished and all that he had become to a big zero.

Imagine.

The tests have been run.

The results are in.

The doctor calls: "It's conclusive. Leprosy. I'm sorry. There's no cure."

What?

There must be a mistake. I'm about to graduate.

This can't be true. We've planned a family vacation. We're going on a cruise for the first time.

No! I'm getting married in six months.

I just received a promotion.

None of that is for you, because what you have is fatal.

All you've worked for . . . all you've become . . . gone with five words.

This is the roadblock that will not only annihilate your dreams—it will take your life as well.

It was Mother's Day when Kelly came face-to-face with that same roadblock. "That's the day my water broke," she says. She and her husband, Tim, were expecting their second child. They had already chosen a name: Tyler Scott Burlington. Labor began early in the day, and she and Tim headed for the hospital.

At 3:09 p.m. Tyler was born. But the day meant for celebration suddenly turned into excruciating grief. "Our son died the day he was born due to heart failure caused by a chromosomal condition called trisomy 18," Kelly says. "We only had two hours to hold our son, take photos and sing to him. Tyler looked like Tim with his distinctive chin, high cheekbones and straight nose."

The physician and hospital staff was compassionate and thoughtful toward the young couple. "Our family and church friends were also an incredible support," Kelly says. "I was 27 years old, and I felt myself slipping into a horrible darkness—something I had never imagined."

***

Death can bulldoze us in the wrong direction faster than a grass hut on fire. Both Kelly and Naaman know the agony and fear of death. We'll catch up with Kelly in a few minutes, but right now let's get back to Naaman.

"Bands of Syrians had invaded the land of Israel, and among their captives was a little girl who had been given to Naaman's wife as a maid." (2 Kings 5:2 LB)

We don't know the name of this girl, but when we research the Scripture, we discover the term "little girl" meant she was old enough to care for a household. So she was probably a teenager. It's likely that Naaman's soldiers had killed her parents during the raid. And now she's a household servant for Naaman's wife.

"One day the little girl said to her mistress, 'I wish my master would go to see the prophet in Samaria. He would heal him of his leprosy!' "
(2 Kings 5:3 LB)

Don't you love her kind heart? She had been taken captive—and though she was in the home of a general and was treated great—she was still a servant. And we can't forget the fact that she's still mourning the death of her parents.

It would have been easy for her to respond an entirely different way to Naaman's leprosy: "Serves you right! You're getting what you deserve."

But her response to her master's leprosy is indicative of her upbringing. We're led to think she lived with parents who had great character and had carefully modeled integrity. We can hear them say, "Do what's right, Honey, even if it's hard."

> Naaman was a five-star general.

She's showing genuine compassion for Naaman and truly wants the best for him. Though she's experienced a lot in her short life, she's definitely on the right road and headed in the right direction. But that doesn't guarantee the pathway will be easy.

"Naaman told the king what the little girl had said." (2 Kings 5:4 LB)

Obviously, this girl lived with such integrity and was so dependable, that her master had great respect for her. Instead of brushing her off with, "You don't know what you're talking about. Stick to your chores." He listened to her. And he took to heart what she said.

"Naaman told the king what the little girl had said. 'Go and visit the prophet,' the king told him. 'I will send a letter of introduction for you to carry to the king of Israel.' " (2 Kings 5:4-5 LB)

Naaman wasn't embarrassed to go to the king with the girl's request. He had such respect for her that he thought her opinion was worthy of the king's attention.

King Ben-Hadad didn't want to lose his right-hand man, so he was eager to do whatever it would take to heal Naaman of leprosy.

"So Naaman started out, taking gifts of $20,000 in silver, $60,000 in gold, and ten suits of clothing."
(2 Kings 5:5 LB)

Travel wasn't easy in those days. Traveling on a donkey—or even behind a chariot—over rocky, dirt roads with the wind sealing grit on your face took determination. But remember Naaman was a sick man. So travel for him was even more difficult. And he was hauling a huge amount of luggage to carry $80,000 worth of gold and silver and a full wardrobe of new clothes.

I remember reading a newspaper article that mentioned most large airports have a physician on call. I thought, *This is great! If I'm ever sick while traveling, I can see the doctor on call.*

About a year later, I was returning home from an international flight and I had a layover in Hong Kong. I was really sick. My throat hurt so bad it felt as though I were swallowing razor blades. I was dizzy and knew my temperature was rising.

I noticed a Burger King in the terminal, so I asked the man behind the counter if the airport had a physician on call. He affirmed they did. I gasped, "Can you please call him?

I'm very sick!"

Within 15 minutes, the physician was there. By this time my fever had spiked to a dangerous temp. I think it was around 99 degrees. And the doctor gave me an incredible medicine. It was called Tylenol.

Okay, you know I'm poking fun at myself, but I'm hammering home the fact that it was hard for me to travel with a sore throat and a low-grade fever even though I was traveling on a nice air-conditioned airplane that glided smoothly through the air. Multiply that times a thousand for Naaman who was traveling with a fatal disease through rugged terrain. It wasn't an easy trip. But at least he's on the right road, and he's going the right direction. He's headed for help. —**Susie**

***

Naaman went straight to the king of Israel with the gifts and King Ben-Hadad's letter.

"The letter to the king of Israel said: 'The man bringing this letter is my servant Naaman; I want you to heal him of his leprosy.' " (2 Kings 5:6 LB)

The king of Israel at this time is Jehoram, son of Ahab. When Johoram receives this letter, he interprets it as a prelude to war. He's shaking in his royal boots.

"When the king of Israel read it, he tore his clothes and said, 'This man sends me a leper to heal! Am I God, that I can kill and give life? He is only trying to get an excuse to invade us again.' " (2 Kings 5:7 LB)

King Ben-Hadad is setting me up, Jehoram is thinking. *He's telling me to heal a leper—when he knows I can't heal anyone! And when Naaman returns home the same way he came, Hadad will start a war with us.*

But the prophet Elisha hears about it and tells Jehoram to send Naaman to him. "This isn't a big deal to God at all," Elisha says. "He can easily heal! And God wants you and Naaman to know that He is God over Israel. So send him to me, and God will use me to show you His power."

"So Naaman arrived with his horses and chariots and stood at the door of Elisha's home. Elisha sent a messenger out to tell him to go and wash in the Jordan River seven times and he would be healed of every trace of his leprosy! But Naaman was angry and stalked away." (2 Kings 5:9-11 LB)

Yes, Naaman had a physical disease that was fatal, but now we see a spiritual disease exhibited in his life, and it's also fatal. It's the disease of pride.

"The LORD detests the proud; they will surely be punished." (Proverbs 16:5 NIV)

Naaman's name actually means "delightful, pleasant, beautiful" and carries the idea of someone who is "well formed." From this information, we can consider that he grew up with the idea that he was God's gift to the world. He was good-looking, well built and carried a dignity and confidence that commanded attention when he entered a room.

So for a man who could have easily been a *GQ* cover guy, having leprosy was not only bad news physically—it was also damaging emotionally and psychologically as well.

Leprosy is known today as Hansen's disease and is now very treatable. But in biblical times, it ruined lives. It was extremely contagious and was spread through skin contact and nose excretions. So if a leper sneezed and you were standing next to him? Bad news! That's why lepers had to shout "Unclean" when out in public. It was a warning for everybody to keep their distance.

Obviously, Naaman's leprosy was in the very beginning stages so he hadn't come to this point yet—but it was simply a matter of time. Leprosy attacked the nervous system. So if someone had leprosy in his foot, he'd lose all feeling in that area. He could walk over broken glass or even have a rusty nail in his foot without knowing it, because he couldn't feel the pain. Infection would set in, and he'd end up losing his foot.

It's been reported that in some undeveloped countries, lepers who had the disease in their hands experienced losing their fingers during their sleep because rats would chew them off. Having leprosy in biblical times was a death sentence. Your body would become disfigured, you'd be an outcast from society, and eventually the disease would take your life.

Back to Naaman.

He was an important man.

So when Elisha didn't even bother to come outside and talk with him—but sent his servant instead—Naaman took his goody-bag and left angry. His pride had been hurt.

" 'Look,' he said, 'I thought at least he would come out and talk to me! I expected him to wave his hand over the leprosy and call upon the name of the Lord his God and heal me! Aren't the Abana River and Pharpar River of Damascus better than all the rivers of Israel put together? If it's rivers I need, I'll wash at home and get rid of my leprosy.' So he went away in a rage."
(2 Kings 5:11-12 LB)

Naaman was also offended that Elisha told him to wash in the Jordan River.

It was filthy.

Vile.

Bacteria-infested.

Muddy.

Not the ideal place to bathe.

So Naaman turns around and heads home. He's now going in the wrong direction. He's heading opposite of where the healing is! Here's the problem: Naaman wants the blessing without having to go through the process. And we often desire the same shortcut. We desire God's blessings, but we want them our way: right now. Immediately!

> The disease of pride can be fatal.

We can skip the process . . . but we won't get the gift. To get the blessing, we must go through the process. What *is* the process? In Naaman's situation it was bathing in the Jordan River. To do that would not only rid him of leprosy, it would eliminate his pride as well.

For us? The process differs with each person. What God is calling you to do will be different from what he's calling your best friend to do. But we can trust that He knows best. Let's leave Naaman in his rage for a moment and catch up with Kelly.

"I think every mother worries that something terrible could happen to her child, but I never truly felt I would have to face the death of *my* child," she says.

The next year was the most difficult time Kelly had ever experienced. Oftentimes she would have remained in bed if it hadn't been for their 18-month-old daughter, Emily. Kelly continued to meet Emily's needs, care for her, love her and comfort her.

"But there were days when I cried nonstop," Kelly says. "And there were times I just got explosively angry. I didn't think life would ever get better again."

***

We can imagine Naaman felt the same way. Why get out of bed when his career and his life were diminishing right before his eyes? The one man who could help him hadn't even come outside to greet him. *Why would I lower myself to wash in that stupid, filthy Jordan?* he must have thought.

But his officers tried to reason with him. "Hey, Naaman, think about it. Washing in the Jordan is a really easy thing to do. It's gross, but it's easy. What if Elisha had told you to climb Mount Everest without any shoes? Or drink a glass of sweat? Or eat 10 pounds of molded bread? As difficult as those things would be, you'd probably do it! So why not go ahead and do this easy thing? Would you really rather suffer with leprosy than smash your pride and bathe in a muddy river and be free?"

Okay, they didn't say it exactly that way. But that's what they meant. Here's how it really went down:

"But his officers tried to reason with him and said, 'If the prophet had told you do some great thing, wouldn't you have done it? So you should certainly obey him when he says simply to go and wash and be cured!'" (2 Kings 5:13 LB)

We, too, want to say, "Come on, Naaman. Turn around. You know the right direction. Submit to the process and receive the blessing."

"So Naaman went down to the Jordan River and dipped himself seven times, as the prophet had told him to. And his flesh became as healthy as a little child's, and he was healed! Then he and his entire party went back to find the prophet; they stood humbly before him and Naaman said, "I know at last that there is no God in all the world except in Israel." (2 Kings 5:15 LB)

When Naaman swallowed his pride and turned around, he experienced the blessing of being healed of leprosy. But before God healed him physically, He wanted to work on his pride. Again, sometimes God wants to take us through a process before He brings us to the blessing.

Flash back to the days of your great-grandparents. If they were Christians, chances are good that when they had a need, they spent time praying about it. And not simply a sentence prayer every day—but they knew how to get on their knees and pray until they prayed through. Most of us don't want to go through that process.

And sometimes after praying for a few weeks and they still didn't have the answer, they may have even added *fasting* to their prayer time. They skipped lunch every day for a week. And instead of eating, they spend that time in prayer instead.

And when they desired to get closer to God, they devoured the Bible. They actually *memorized* Scripture. They participated in a Bible study. And when their pastor preached about having a burden for lost souls, they shared their faith and invited non-Christian co-workers and neighbors to church. Again, many of us don't want to go through all of that. We offer fast prayers, and we want quick answers.

But oftentimes, God works through process. And again, we can skip the process, but we'll forfeit the blessing.

> Oftentimes, God works through process.

Naaman finally submitted to the process and experienced the blessing of healing and being divinely redirected. You see, before going through this process, Naaman would have never admitted that Israel's God was more important than himself. But now he's making a proclamation: "I know at last that there is no God in all the world except in Israel." This isn't simply about head knowledge; this is about heart knowledge.

Naaman was healed.

But he was also transformed from the inside out.

He's returning home as a believer.

He's been converted.

And from this point on, he'll never worship a foreign god.

". . . from now on I will never again offer any burnt offerings or sacrifices to any other god except the Lord." (2 Kings 5:17 LB)

God has completely redirected Naaman's life!
What about Kelly?

Kelly's husband was pastoring a church full of people who were trying to reach out to their pastor's wife, but they didn't know the depth of her depression and sometimes felt helpless.

"But after a year," Kelly says, "in the midst of my darkness, cracks began to appear, and light slowly started to shine through. I knew God was speaking love to me. I knew He was asking me to trust Him.

"It was certainly a process," she says. "But in the deepest human pain I have ever known, I felt a comfort and peace begin to overtake the sadness and despair. God's presence and love became a reality for me," she says. "My confidence in my Redeemer was coming back. I saw Him divinely redirecting my life.

"I can't adequately put into words how God changed me as I grieved for my son. And again, it was definitely a process. The most difficult time for me emotionally became the most special time for me spiritually!"

Kelly refused to let the despair and depression win. Her marriage became stronger, her outlook on life grew more grateful, and she developed a more patient style of parenting.

"If we'll put our faith in God, He will rush to meet us at our exact point of need. He is close to the brokenhearted! He rescues those who feel crushed in their spirit. Christ saved me from living the rest of my life in darkness and hopelessness.

"This is what I've learned from the brief life of my son: Hope is a beautiful thing. Faith gives strength. And love that comes from God can defeat any darkness or fear. Yes, it's sometimes a process, but there is blessing on the other side."

***

Both Naaman and Kelly allowed God to redirect their lives. And sometimes that redirection requires allowing Christ to take us through a tough learning process. But during that process is when He gently removes things that hinder us such as pride, depression, anger—and even shame.

Please turn to the study section on page 187. After you're finished, we'll see how God can rescue those who are trapped in a web of shame.

Chapter Eight

Redirection from Shame

Vivian married a 28-year-old man named Mike when she was just 17. He began drinking only a few months after their marriage, and she found herself entangled inside a web of abuse.

"He forbade me and our little girl to attend church, and I felt spiritually starved," Vivian says. "Mike punched and slapped me, and he also told me I was fat and called me all kinds of derogatory names. He isolated me and wouldn't allow me to see my friends or family. The toll of physical abuse on my body and verbal and emotional abuse on my mind weighed heavily on me. Though I didn't have much strength left, I had enough to finally divorce him after three long, agonizing years."

Vivian married again a year later. "Travis also began abusing me shortly after we were married. He had a short fuse, and it was easy for him to become violent very quickly.

"Travis back-handed me, held me down, grabbed my face and even cut me with glass. One night he fractured my cheekbone. He was extremely manipulative. And although the physical abuse was terrible, the verbal abuse was much worse.

"He made it clear that he didn't believe in God; therefore he didn't believe in heaven or hell, either. Because of this, he was never concerned about consequences to his abuse. He beat me black and blue, and as his drinking escalated, so did the abuse."

Why didn't Vivian leave him? "When he wasn't abusing me, we had an okay life. We always had nice things, he worked hard, we took family vacations, and he attended the kids' sporting events. I went to college and earned two degrees, we were making good money, and we had a nice place to live. For once in my life, I was physically fit, loved my job and felt good about myself. It was only when he was drinking that things were violent. He could go a few years at a time without drinking, but when he *did* drink, it was horrific."

Vivian and Travis were married 16 years until he was killed in a tragic motorcycle wreck. A few years later, Vivian met Kevin. "I finally started seeking God's direction and making good decisions," she says. "I had to overcome a lot of shame for bad choices in my past. I'm now surrounded by an amazing group of people in my church who love me, a husband who cherishes me, and I'm growing consistently closer to my heavenly Father. With a lot of prayer and Christian friendships, He is healing the shame and teaching me to see myself through His eyes."

***

The road of shame is a difficult journey. Tamar traveled this boulevard way back in 1,000 BC.

Who's Tamar?

She was the daughter of King David who ruled Israel for 40 years. The Bible describes her as beautiful: **"Tamar ... the beautiful sister of Absalom son of David."** (2 Samuel 13:1 NIV)

This young princess had everything going for her: status, wealth and influence. But all that would unexpectedly change one fateful morning. To set the scene, we need to read 2 Samuel 13:1 in its entirety. Here it is:

"In the course of time, Amnon son of David fell in love with Tamar, the beautiful sister of Absalom son of David."

There are several weak links in this royal family's dysfunction, and we see some of the dysfunction here in the fact that David had several wives. We're told in Genesis 2:24 that one man and one woman shall become two—not one man and lots of women. And Deuteronomy 17:14-20 specifically says that all kings are to have only one wife.

> What culture deems normal doesn't mean it's right.

But having several wives was simply part of their culture. It had become "normal" in their society. What culture deems as *normal* doesn't mean it's *right*. Polygamy has always been wrong in God's eyes.

So this family chain is a weak one.

And Amnon fell in love with his half-sister Tamar.

The Bible says he fell in love—but it was more like he fell in LUST for her.

Many of us confuse lust with love.

Lust has a lot more to do with hormones than it has to do with love or respect. And when lust combines with arrogance, shame and the need for power—the result is often rape.

Amnon was so in lust with Tamar that he made himself ill. It seemed that he could do nothing about his lust but fantasize about her. Then Amnon's cousin came up with a plan. Let's look at the Scripture:

"Prince Absalom, David's son, had a beautiful sister named Tamar.

"And Prince Amnon (her half-brother) fell desperately in love with her. Amnon became so tormented by his love for her that he became ill.

"He had no way of talking to her, for the girls and young men were kept strictly apart.

"But Amnon had a very crafty friend—his cousin Jonadab (the son of David's brother Shimeah).

"One day Jonadab said to Amnon, 'What's the trouble? Why should the son of a king look so haggard morning after morning?'

"So Amnon told him, 'I am in love with Tamar, my half-sister.'

" 'Well,' Jonadab said, 'I'll tell you what to do. Go back to bed and pretend you are sick; when your father comes to see you, ask him to let Tamar come and prepare some food for you. Tell him you'll feel better if she feeds you.'

"So Amnon did. And when the king came to see him, Amnon asked him for this favor—that his sister Tamar be permitted to come and cook a little something for him to eat.

"David agreed and sent word to Tamar to go to Amnon's quarters and prepare some food for him.

"So she did and went into his bedroom so that he could watch her mix some dough; then she baked some special bread for him.

"But when she set the serving tray before him, he refused to eat! 'Everyone get out of here,' he told his servants; so they all left the apartment."
(2 Samuel 13:1-9 NIV)

Amnon's wicked plan is coming together.

"Then Amnon said to Tamar, 'Bring the food here into my bedroom so I may eat from your hand.'

"And Tamar took the bread she had prepared and brought it to her brother Amnon in his bedroom.

"But when she took it to him to eat, he grabbed her and said, 'Come to bed with me, my sister.'

" 'No, my brother!' she said to him.' "
(2 Samuel 13:10-12 LB)

Let's just stop here for a moment and make sure we all know this FACT: Any sexual contact that happens after someone has said NO is considered rape.

Continuing with Scripture:

"But he refused to listen to her, and since he was stronger than she, he raped her.

"Then Amnon hated her with intense hatred. In fact, he hated her more than he had loved her."
(2 Samuel 13:14 LB)

So when Amnon is finished, he's seized with great loathing for her. He was disgusted with her. He got what he wanted, and now he couldn't care less about Tamar.

"Amnon said to her, 'Get up and get out!' " (2 Samuel 13:15 LB)

Amnon wants her out. "Get up and get out!" Did you notice he's not even using her name? He has robbed her of her identify.

Actually, in the original Hebrew, Amnon says, "Get THIS out of here."

He no longer even views her as a person! He has not only robbed Tamar of her identity; he has also robbed her of her humanity.

Tamar is now seen by her culture as damaged goods.

> Don't let your identity be defined by what happened to you in the past.

Perhaps you remember the television game show "The Weakest Link." It debuted in America on April 16, 2001. The hostess was the sharp-tongued British woman Anne Robinson. The fear of being on this game show was having Anne point her finger at you and deliver the scathing, "You ARE the weakest link!" accusation in front of millions of viewers. She had a stern schoolmistress demeanor about her, and her British brogue delivered the verdict with acerbic authority.

It's with this same abrasive ruling that society labels Tamar. In arduous eruption, her culture screams, "Tamar! YOU ARE the weakest link!"

"You're no good!"

"You're worthless."

Maybe you can identify.

Perhaps there have been times when you, too, have felt like the weakest link. Damaged. Used. Or abused.

The Bible says she spent the rest of her years lonely and desolate.

But the story doesn't end here. Tamar's brother Absalom asked her what had happened—even though he already suspected that Amnon had violated her. Then Absalom added to her shame by saying this:

" **'Be quiet for now, my sister; he is your brother. Don't take this thing to heart.'** " (2 Samuel 13:20 NIV)

Her brother Absalom loved his sister, Tamar, but he couldn't bring restoration to her. In her own mind, she was damaged goods.

Although Tamar was a daughter of the king, she lived the rest of her life in shame and as a desolate woman.

Tamar was an innocent victim.

Something bad happened to her that wasn't her fault.

Does this sound familiar?

Can you relate?

Maybe you, too, have been the recipient of something bad that wasn't your fault. Perhaps you know what it's like to have your identity shaped in shame.

Ron knows exactly what that's like. He lived with shame for decades.

I've lived with shame for years. I was severely abused by my father. Allow me to start at the beginning. I'm the first-born to Charles and Ruth. At the time of my birth, my father was a new Christian and a budding preacher in a very strict Pentecostal church.

My mother is the youngest of 10, and her family was involved in the United Pentecostal Church. Her grandfather was even a pastor in this denomination.

A few years after I was born, my father walked away from church. The knight in shining armor that my mother thought she married turned into a living nightmare.

He was a rageaholic—a man full of hurt and anger. He became physically abusive to my mother and later to me. When my baby sister was born—seven years younger than me—my father began an affair with the woman who served as Mother's nurse during the birth process. This affair continues today—56 years later.

As I entered my teen years, his rage intensified and became fixated on me physically and verbally. He stopped calling me by my name and referred to me as "You dumb son of a b—."

When I was in the eighth grade, he took me to our barn, removed the reins off of a horse bridle and beat me with them. I had bruises and whelps from the back of my neck to the bend in my knees. He only stopped when my mother physically intervened—and then he beat her until she was bloodied.

In eighth grade PE, we showered after class, and as the coach was handing out towels he saw the evidence of the beating. I remember getting on my knees and begging him not to call the police because I knew my father would do it again. Surprisingly, the coach didn't report it.

I had such hatred toward my father that I even fantasized about killing him, but I knew that God had a higher calling on my life. At age 12, I answered the call to ministry. I often wondered if my dad had been abused himself. I had even heard a rumor that his three sisters had sexually abused him. Just a few years ago, I asked him about it. His reply was stunning: "Abused? No, but they had sex with me frequently." That was proof of how skewed his view of normalcy was.

My Turning Point

I attended a Christian university where I studied counseling. I knew the Holy Spirit was working inside of my damaged emotions, but I also knew it would be a long process. As I wrote my doctoral thesis, God brought several wonderful people into my life who began pouring into my healing. At age 40, I began to see a therapist and finally saw the beginnings of a breakthrough.

One major part of my healing has come through my wonderful Christian wife and children who consistently loved and affirmed me as a man, husband and father.

A huge roadblock for me was the phrase in the Lord's prayer, "Our Father who art in heaven." When I stopped arguing with God over the father issue and simply accepted Him as Father, my brokenness began to change.

Though I'll never be able to forget my past, I have certainly given it to God. He can use it for His glory. My mother passed away a few years ago, and my father is still a messed-up, broken, angry man involved in a variety of affairs.

God has miraculously removed the shame from my life and given me an incredible ministry as the senior pastor of a church in New York. He completely turned my life around. He changed my emotional direction. And now I see Him working every day in my life. I'm blessed that He has chosen to use me to be a catalyst for healing in the lives of so many others who are broken.

***

What happened to Tamar couldn't change her bloodline—she was still the daughter of the king—but she lived the rest of her life believing she was the weakest link. She believed she was broken . . . unwhole. Now she's living with no hope. She's allowing her identity to be shaped by shame instead of the fact that her daddy is the king. Scripture tells us she spent the rest of her life in loneliness and despair outside of King David's home.

But she *could* have lived in the palace!

If only she would have looked up instead of down.

If she had looked up, she would have seen God refuting the weakest link syndrome.

Wouldn't you love to pause the story and say, "Tamar! You are NOT damaged goods! In God's chain, there ARE no weak links. You're still a princess. You're still the daughter of the king. Live like it!"

You see God is in the restoration business.

> You are the object of God's love.

He's a Master at taking weak and broken links and making them whole.

He's not simply into recovery; He's into complete and total restoration!

He wants to restore us, and He wants to TRANSFORM us! How?

#1: By not conforming to the pattern of this world.

Let's go to the Bible:

"Do not conform to the pattern of this world, but be transformed." (Romans 12:2 NIV)

Refuse to believe the lies of the world around you! Tamar believed the lies of her culture.

Okay, God wants to renew, restore and transform me. But how?

By not conforming to the pattern of this world.

But how do I do that?

How do I keep from conforming to the world around me? How do I NOT believe the lies the world is shouting to me?

We get the answer in the rest of Romans 12:2. THIS is how God transforms us.

#2: "Do not conform to the pattern of this world, but be transformed *by the renewing of your mind."* (Romans 12:2 NIV)

Being transformed by the renewing of our mind is done by the Holy Spirit as He teaches us who we really are.

So who are you?

Who are you . . . *really?*

How about asking your Creator?

Let God tell you who you are!

Check out what Jesus says to the apostle Peter:

" 'And now I'm going to tell you who you are, *really* are.' " (Matthew 16:17 The Message)

Have you allowed God to shape your identity?

Is your identity grounded in Him?

According to Scripture, it not only *can* be; it *should* be:

"Therefore, if anyone is in Christ, he is a new creation. The old has passed away; behold, the new has come." (2 Corinthians 5:17 ESV)

Wouldn't it be great to take Tamar out for a Frappuccino and say, "Tamar, what was done to you was terrible. But it's in the past. Behold! The new has come, Tamar! Don't let your identity be defined by what happened to you. Define yourself in Christ!"

You see, we tend to think God only likes us when we're doing good things, or when we're being good.

And this is the *number one lie of the enemy*. He hisses, "This thing is about your performance—not the Cross."

No.

No!

NO.

Because the Bible stories look like it's way more about Jesus than my behavior.

Who Am I?

You are the object of God's love!

He's crazy about you!

In the Old Testament, He says in Zephaniah 3:17 that He sings a song over you! And chances are good that it's an individual song He wrote just for you.

In other words, the song He sings over you doesn't sound anything like the song He's singing over your family members and friends. The song He created for you is unique—it has your DNA, your tastes, your chromosomal structure and your rhythm entwined within the notes.

That's not all! In Isaiah 49:16, we're told that God has engraved you in the palm of His hand.

No, He didn't quickly jot your name on His hand like a phone number He hopes He won't forget. He didn't write your name with a Bic pen that can be easily washed away. Nor did He use a Sharpie that will eventually fade with time.

He has *engraved* you in the palm of His hand.

YOU. And it's not just your name . . . it's *you*.

The essence of you.

Who you are.

Okay, if He didn't use a pen or a Sharpie, what's my name written with? Something close to a railroad spike. Yes, He was thinking of you when the spikes went through His palms.

YOU are the object of God's love.

Let that transform your mind!

Sounds good, but . . . I need more.

Okay.

You can know you're the object of God's love because He sings a song over you every day of your life—and because you're engraved in the palm of His hand—and also because Jesus prays for you!

Did you know that? In John 17, Jesus began praying for you even before you were born!

And guess what.

When Jesus prays, He gets His prayers answered!

We can be confident that Jesus answers His own prayers.

And Jesus carries the theme of this prayer to the Upper Room where He meets with His disciples. He really wants them to get this. It's of utmost importance that they get this. It's imperative that they get this. They *must* get it. It's crucial. The future of Christianity will depend on it.

Here's the scene. Jesus climbs the stairs into the upper room. The disciples are waiting for Him to begin what will be their last supper together on earth. Jesus gazes into their eyes.

"Hey! Guys! Look at Me. Peter stop talking for a second. Look at Me. Matthew, put the money down. Look at Me. Thomas, stop doubting. Look at Me. Bartholomew, pay attention. Here it is:

"As Father God loves Me . . . that is *exactly* how I love you!

Get it?

You are NOT the weakest link!

You are the object of God's love!

I love *you* EXACTLY how the Father loves Me."

Oh, may this truth infuse your lives!
Let it saturate your being.

Can you hear His voice? He's saying the same thing to you through these pages. Jesus is telling you right here . . . right now . . . that just as the Father loves Him, so HE LOVES YOU!

Wow.

Let that transform your mind.

Let that truth erase the shame.

Recap

How can I be transformed?

#1: "Don't conform to the pattern of this world." (Romans 12:2)

The culture is spreading lies about you. Satan says you're defeated, worthless, damaged, shameful, broken and the weakest link.

Well, that's what we used to be. But when we come to Christ, everything changes. So refuse to conform to the lies and pattern of the world around you any longer. You are a new creation!

#2: "Be transformed by the renewing of your mind." (Romans 12:2 NIV)

You're a child of the King.

You're the object of God's love.

Christ loves you—just as Father God loves Him.

Jesus really really really really REALLY wants you to get this!

The apostle John got it! He was the only disciple not martyred.

King Domitian tried to boil John alive, and when that didn't work—he banished him to the criminally infested, rocky island of Patmos. There was never enough to eat. The conditions were deplorable. And that's where John wrote the book of Revelation.

He also wrote First, Second and Third John. And when he wrote the Gospel of John, he didn't even use his name; he simply referred to himself as "the disciple whom Jesus loved."

He got it!

It's as though you hear him shouting between the lines of his gospel account: "Jesus loves ME the very same way that

God the Father and Creator of the universe and the Great I AM loves Him!"

And THAT became his identity.

This was the very core of his being.

His identity could have easily been in what he did. He could have said, "Hey! I helped lead the church in Ephesus. I wrote five books in the New Testament. I'm writing the very last book of the Bible—the one that tells the future!"

Surely John could have found identity in his success. He could have easily developed a cool factor. But it's as though he's saying, "Nope. I'm not going to write about who I know or what I've done.

"This Book—the Bible—is probably going to be a big seller. But here's how I want it to go down. Just remember me this way: the disciple whom Jesus loved."

Who Are You?

If you're asking *who am I?* You're much more than a career person, a wife, a husband, a mom, a dad, a student, a teen, a caring friend—that's not the core of who you are!

And if you're basing your identity on what happened to you in the past—and if you're living in shame, regret or embarrassment—you're missing the point.

Your identity isn't shame.

You are not defined by your past.

If you're asking "Who am I? What's my identity?"

Here it is: YOU are the disciple whom Jesus loves! And how does He love you? He loves you exactly like God the Father loves Him.

Wow.

THAT'S your identity.

You are NOT the weakest link.
You are not damaged goods.
You are not broken.
You are not what society deems you to be.
Your name isn't "shame."
You're a child of the King.
You have access to His Kingdom.
You are engraved in the Palm of His hand.

Go ahead. Say it out loud:
"I am the disciple whom Jesus loves exactly as God loves Him.
This is who I am.
This is the very fiber of my being.
This is my core.
I am the disciple Jesus loves!"

When you know that—truly know that—you don't care as much about what others say. And the fact that something happened to you that you didn't have control of begins to fade away, because you know who you are! And you become TRANSFORMED by that truth!

Do you know what that transformation does? It not only erases shame, but it turns your whole life around. It divinely redirects you.

To continue processing all you've just read, go directly to the study section on page 189. Then we'll take a peek at how freeing it is to be transformed and divinely redirected from deceit and selfishness.

Chapter Nine
Redirection from Self

Are you familiar with the television game show "The Price Is Right?" It first aired in 1957. Seventy-four games are consistently rotated on the show. The biggest prize anyone has won on the daily show is a black Audi R8 convertible worth $157,300.

In 2003, "The Price Is Right" aired three primetime evening specials, and the most someone won during one of these episodes was $1,153,908 in cash and prizes.

But the Bible actually records people who played this game centuries ago. Let's meet the contestants: Jacob and Esau. (They could have also starred on "Family Feud," but today we find them in the audience for "The Price Is Right.")

Before we get to know the stars of our show, let's meet their parents: Isaac and Rebekah. Isaac was 40 years old when he married Rebekah, and when we open Genesis 25, we see Isaac pleading with God for his wife, because she was barren. God responded, and Rebekah became pregnant with twins. Isaac was 60 when they had fraternal twin boys.

A Tale of Two Brothers

The contention between these boys actually began in the womb and would continue throughout their years. Fraternal doesn't even begin to describe the extreme differences between these twins. Esau was born with thick red hair. His name means *hairy*.

His twin, Jacob, was born with his hand on Esau's heel. This is how he got his name: Jacob, *'One who takes the heel'* or *'heel-grabber.'* It defines him. If he were a professional wrestler this would be his signature move. Having older parents and names such as Hairy and Heel Grabber, puts them off to a rough start.

Esau was an outdoorsman. Many days were spent in pursuit of his prey and many nights under a blanket of stars. He mastered the hunt. And, because of this, Isaac had a special place in his heart for Esau. He was a daddy's boy.

Jacob's idea of camping was cozying up inside of a Holiday Inn complete with a free cookie at check-in. Scripture tells us he stayed among the tents; he was a homebody. Jacob was closer to his mom and enjoyed indoor hobbies.

He took special interest in the domestic side of things. His tools were pots and pans. He yearned for the Good Housekeeping Seal of Approval. Though we'll soon view him on "The Price Is Right," he could have also been a competitor on "Top Chef."

> Every believer in Christ has a birthright.

Though Jacob and Esau were polar opposites, they shared a strong controlling characteristic: They were extremely self-consumed.

When self-centeredness rears its' ugly head, it destroys. Being self-centered creates a tsunami of devastation that quickly ruins family relationships and fractures friendships. The consequence of being self-consumed is loss, sorrow and emptiness.

Here's What's Happening

The Bible gives us two settings to describe the scene between Esau and Jacob:

Setting one: We find Esau on a hunting trip.

Setting two: We see Jacob thumbing through the recipe books. He's making stew.

The settings soon meld together to create the unfolding scene in Scripture:

"The boys grew up, and Esau became a skillful hunter, a man of the open country, while Jacob was content to stay at home among the tents.

"Isaac, who had a taste for wild game, loved Esau, but Rebekah loved Jacob.

"Once when Jacob was cooking some stew, Esau came in from the open country, famished.

"He said to Jacob, 'Quick, let me have some of that red stew! I'm famished!'

"Jacob replied, 'First sell me your birthright.'

" 'Look, I am about to die,' Esau said. 'What good is the birthright to me?'

"But Jacob said, 'Swear to me first.' So he swore an oath to him, selling his birthright to Jacob.

"Then Jacob gave Esau some bread and some lentil stew. He ate and drank, and then got up and left. So Esau despised his birthright" (Genesis 25:27-34 NIV)

The Game Show

And now standing center stage and directly in the spotlight, we see Jacob and Esau playing "The Price Is Right." What is Esau's bid for the price of his birthright?

A bowl of stew.

Though he won the stew, he actually lost the prize.

Let's dig a little deeper.

According to Old Testament law, as owner of the birthright, the oldest son would receive a double inheritance (Deuteronomy 21:17). He would also assume the spiritual leadership of the family—making sure the family was taken care of financially and that they walked with God spiritually. In other words, as priest of the home, he would have a significant role to play in ministry.

In watching Esau's negotiating skills on "The Price Is Right," we can see that he would have made an A+ in drama class:

"I'm famished. I'm dying! Give me some stew. NOW!"

Esau didn't trade his birthright because he was so hungry that he was about to die, or because there wasn't anything else to eat in the house, but because he wanted to fulfill the desires of the flesh.

He was self-consumed.

Esau was willing to trade his entire spiritual heritage for a whim of the moment.

He devoured the bowl of soup without giving another thought to his birthright. It meant nothing to him. Esau couldn't care less about ministry. He refused to delay his gratification.

Right Here, Right Now

Don't we see the same thing happening today?
We want instant gratification.
This is why so many are in financial debt.
Gotta buy new furniture NOW.
Gotta have a new car NOW.

Isn't instant gratification the reason so many people are sexually involved outside of marriage? Gotta have my desires met NOW.

In today's culture, delayed gratification is almost unknown.

If we want it, we can get it.

Order it on Amazon NOW. And if you're a prime member, get it by tomorrow! Instant gratification is a sign of being self-consumed.

And there are always consequences. Eric experienced this first-hand:

My Dad was a pastor, so I was in church every time the doors were open. When I was in elementary school, I felt God's call on my life to become a fulltime minister, so I planned my life in that direction. My teen years were spent dreaming of becoming a pastor.

Fast-forward a few years: After I was in the ministry about 15 years, I became disillusioned because of the hypocrisy and ugliness I saw in the church. I began questioning if I'd ever even seen God truly do anything in my life.

I became selfish and started blaming God. I remember asking Him, "Why are You doing this to me when I've given You all my life?"

I focused more and more on myself—*my* needs, *my* desires, *my* questions—until my marriage fell apart. I left the ministry and selfishly decided that following God just didn't work for me.

Full Speed Downward

When I left God, I totally walked away. I overindulged in all things opposite of Christ's plan. I lived a life of debauchery and perversion. I tried about everything and anything including excessive drinking and sexual experimentation.

I married a woman who was also a runaway from God, and together we fed our addictions for anything we thought would satisfy. We opened up our marriage to the ravages of the enemy all while trying to begin a life together. Eventually we even tried to bring in a "sister-wife" to live with us, because we thought we had evolved to a state of open-mindedness.

After 10 years of living the life of a self-absorbed prodigal, my life crumbled. I lost a job because of my lifestyle, and my wife was angry with our crazy messed-up marriage. I was devastated and desperate.

I thought about running away to someplace really far where no one would know me and no one could find me. I also considered ending my life. I thought my wife and children would be able to finally succeed if I weren't pulling them down. It was the lowest point in my life that I've ever experienced. Totally dark is the only way I know how to describe this.

What Do I Really Want?

In the middle of all this darkness, my wife found someone else and was ready to leave me. This got my attention! I allowed God to begin demolishing the walls I had built between my life and anything holy.

God also began dealing with my wife. It was an extremely slow process for her to see that I was truly ready to change and get serious about Christ. I was very low during this time as well. I had come back to God but didn't want to have to pay the cost of the consequences I was experiencing. I just wanted everything to magically be okay.

But I had hurt so many people—as well as broken the heart of my Savior—I knew I'd have to pay the price of getting my life back together. I want to be careful that I'm not misunderstood. God forgave me wholly, and I knew He wiped my slate clean. But because of the selfish choices I'd made, I needed to make things right with people. That's the cost.

So we began seeing a counselor, and we got diligently involved in Celebrate Recovery. These were high costs to me, because they forced me to deal with pride. I had to humble myself to admit I needed help—and a lot of help!

On the Other Side

Through the prayers of family and help from pastors, we survived. We have allowed God to transform our lives. It's hard to see that we're the same people who once were so lost.

I won't be able to pastor again, but I'm finding that God can use me to minister wherever He leads me. I'm a fulltime high school teacher and coach, and my wife is a nurse. We love our church and are involved in our Sunday school class, and we still attend Celebrate Recovery when we can.

I'm a living testimony of the fact that God is more than able to transform a self-consumed life and use it for His glory.

***

Your Birthright

Every believer in Christ has a birthright. Every believer in Christ has special privileges, because we are considered "firstborn" sons of God.

Warning: Refuse to trade your privileges for momentary pleasures. Determine not to exchange something of infinite value for instant thrills. There are consequences for playing "The Price Is Right" with God's calling on your life.

Before we leave Esau to catch up with Jacob, let's recap the importance of the birthright:

- The man who had the birthright was in contact with God, and he was priest of the family.
- He was the man who had a covenant *from* God.
- He had a relationship *with* God.

So in effect, Esau said, "I'd rather have a bowl of soup than have a relationship with God."

That's frightening.

But . . . don't we say the same thing every time we put something before God?

"I have too much work to do, so I'll skip church."

"I'm too busy to read the Bible."

"I really need some time at the lake—away from ministry, away from spiritual responsibilities, away from . . . God?"

Closer to Home

Can we get invasively honest right now?

Could it be . . . that you're traded your spiritual birthright? Have you sold your spiritual responsibilities—not accepted ministry involvement—because you wanted something else more? "I *would* get more involved in church, but I don't want to tie myself down. I want the freedom to (fill in the blank)."

As believers, we have two natures within us, and they're struggling against each other. Paul describes this battle in Galatians 5:19-21:

> As believers, we have two natures within us, and they're struggling against each other.

"But when you follow your own wrong inclinations, your lives will produce these evil results:
impure thoughts,
eagerness for lustful pleasure,
idolatry,
spiritism (that is, encouraging the activity of demons),
hatred and fighting,
jealousy and anger,
constant effort to get the best for yourself,
complaints and criticisms,
the feeling that everyone else is wrong except those in your own little group—
and there will be wrong doctrine,
envy, murder, drunkenness, wild parties,

and all that sort of thing.

Let me tell you again, as I have before, that anyone living that sort of life will not inherit the Kingdom of God." (LB)

This is living in the flesh.

This is playing "The Price Is Right" and trading how God wants us to live with how Satan wants us to live.

But here's God's prize. This is how He wants us to live. He offers us this showcase:

"But when the Holy Spirit controls our lives he will produce this kind of fruit in us:

love,

   joy,

      peace,

         patience,

            kindness,

               goodness,

                  faithfulness,

                     gentleness

                        and self-control."

                            (Galatians 5:22-23 LB)

The Holy Spirit wants to manifest all nine fruit in your life.

If you're not experiencing one of the nine fruits, it's because you've traded it for one of the fleshly qualities. You can use these two paragraphs in your Bible as a checklist.

Look at Galatians 5:22-23 that describe the fruit of the Spirit, and circle anything you're *not* experiencing. Then read the paragraph above it that describes the sins of the flesh (or the carnal nature) and circle the one that has canceled-out the fruit you're not experiencing.

It works every time.

Example: Not experiencing peace?

Look at the paragraph above it: Jealousy, fighting, criticism. Are you battling one of these? If so, it has canceled-out peace.

Are you not experiencing joy?

Look at the paragraph above it: Anger.

That would certainly negate the joy in your life.

It's an excellent checklist. Use it!

Refuse to play "The Price Is Right" with how God wants you to live. There's just not a price that's worth it. And by doing so, you soon find yourself headed in the wrong direction.

As we've discovered in other situations, God can certainly redirect your path, but there can be some difficult consequences. For Esau? He never received all that was rightfully his.

Heel Grabber

Let's chat about Jacob.

Jacob was a deceiver, but he also had a spiritual discernment that his brother didn't share. We've seen that Esau was a man of the flesh and didn't care for spiritual things.

Jacob was at the very least opportunistic. He pounced on his brother's weakness. Esau didn't wake him up at midnight asking for something to eat. Jacob was already stirring the pot. The soup was ready.

His hungry brother who had been hunting since dawn really *is* weak, and he's light-headed with hunger. No, he's not going to die. But he's standing next to the pot of bubbling soup.

He can see it.

    He can smell it.

        And he wants some.

How easy it would have been for Jacob to simply give him some soup.

But Jacob is self-centered. He, too, has chosen to head in the wrong direction of where God wants him to be spiritually. He's obsessed with Esau's birthright. He has desired it his entire life. He wants it more than anything.

So he says, "You're famished? I have a huge bowl of soup that's piping hot, and it has your name on it! All you have to do is sign over your birthright."

This is vintage Jake. We're seeing a clear demonstration of his true nature. Several places in Scripture have painted him as a smart deceiver. Later, he'll trick his father, Isaac, into releasing the birthright to him. And a few years down the road, he'll con his uncle Laban. Jacob knew the value of the birthright, and he wanted it for himself.

But God had already gone on record saying, "The elder shall serve the younger" (Genesis 25:23). When the boys were in their mother's womb, an angel had told Rebekah that the firstborn would serve his twin.

But Jacob didn't want to wait on the Lord.

Rather than trust in God's Word,

    God's timing,

        God's ways,

             Jacob took matters into his own hands.

He was desperate to be a contestant on "The Price Is Right."

The Flesh

We see a similar battle raging inside of Jacob that raged inside of Esau, don't we? Jacob knew what he wanted. He knew what he valued. And instead of waiting on the Lord and allowing things to happen God's way, Jacob's fleshly nature took over. Like Esau, he too, was obsessed with instant gratification due to being self-consumed. He wanted the instant gratification of grasping the birthright.

Isn't this a battle we all fight?

The apostle Paul reminds us in 2 Corinthians 10 that we're not to walk in the flesh! Let's look at Jesus' own words:

"For what does it profit a man to gain the whole world and forfeit his soul." (Mark 8:36 ESV)

And **". . . is anything worth more than his soul?"** (Mark 8:37 LB)

When we allow ourselves to become attracted to things of the world, we're tempted to reach for them instead of focusing on our soul. Contemporary Christian artist TobyMac sings about this in his song "Lose My Soul."

Personal Gain

Jacob became a ruthless man. "First, sell me your birthright." Esau only wanted a bowl of the cheapest bean stew. It was the food of peasants. Jacob's price for giving it to his brother was sky high: Esau's birthright. He saw Esau's weakness and used it for his own personal gain.

Are we sometimes guilty of the same?

You may have heard religious people who claim to have the gift of healing the sick, but they require "seed-faith money" before the healing will take place. Why wouldn't they say, "Freely we have received this gift of healing from God, and so freely we give!

Did Jesus ever set a price before He gave sight to the blind or cleansing for the leper? Do we ever see Jesus seek personal gain throughout Scripture? We *do* see Him model selflessness. But we never see self-centeredness.

How much did each one of the 5,000 men have to pay to have loaves and fish in abundance for supper (John 6:1-14)?

Not a penny.

It was all free.

And what about the price for eternal life?

> Self-centeredness will always lead us in the wrong direction.

"Just as I am without one plea" . . . and He accepts you just as you are. (See Romans 10:9-10, 1 John 3:16.)

Fast-Forward

Let's move on with Jacob's life.

We see him in an all-night wrestling match in Genesis 32:22-32. He wins the battle, but there are consequences to the fight: He walks with a limp the rest of his life.

Let's fast-forward again on Jacob's life. He's now an old man, and his next-to-youngest son, Joseph, is in high standing with Pharaoh. Through Joseph's leadership, he has saved Egypt from the great famine that has swept the land. Joseph's older brothers, who once betrayed him, bring their father, Jacob, to Joseph for food and shelter.

Joseph, in turn, introduces his father to Pharaoh. Let's eavesdrop on Jacob and Pharaoh's conversation:

"Then Joseph brought in his father, Jacob, and presented him to Pharaoh. And Jacob blessed Pharaoh.

" 'How old are you?' Pharaoh asked him.

"Jacob replied, 'I have traveled this earth for 130 hard years. But my life has been short compared to the lives of my ancestors.' " (Genesis 47:9 NLT)

In other words, "I have a lot materially, but it's been an extremely hard life."

Oh, Jacob! Your life could have been lived in victory if you'd trusted God to work out *His* plan in your life instead of trying to work things your way.

Yes, Jacob was grateful God had intervened in his life and turned him around. But he still lived with the consequences of some poor choices.

Lessons Learned?

What can we glean from these twin brothers?

God *wants* to save us from self-centeredness.

God *can* save us from self-centeredness.

God *will* save us from self-centeredness—if we'll allow Him to redirect our focus. But the longer we head in the wrong direction, the greater the consequences.

Esau's life was changed forever because of the deceptive choices his brother made. Though we serve a God of forgiveness, it's our responsibility to make things right with those we have harmed. The Bible shows Jacob did this in Genesis chapters 32-33. It wasn't easy, and Jacob still carried the heaviness of his poor choices the rest of his life.

Can you identify with Jacob? Have you tried to work out God's plan in your own strength, doing things your own way—even to the extent to taking advantage of someone? "I *can* make it work. I *will* make it work." Have relationships been damaged because of poor choices you now regret?

Perhaps you see a bit of Esau in you. Have you put other things above God's very best for your life . . . in essence selling your birthright for temporary pleasure?

Could it be that you've been playing "The Price Is Right" with God? If so, He invites you to walk away from the game.

Self-sufficiency,
    self-centeredness,
        and self-consummation will always keep us from becoming whom God desires us to be. And it will always lead us in the wrong direction.

God isn't into games.

He *is* into complete fulfillment.

Consider completing the study section on page 191. And then let's dive inside the reality of your amazing *tomorrow!*

Chapter Ten
Redirection for Tomorrow

Grab your passports and buckle your seatbelts.
We're traveling back in time.
The year: A.D. 33.
The place: Golgotha—a skull-shaped hill in Jerusalem.
The event: It's Passover Friday. Jesus has been crucified.

As we take an inside view of this day—and the days preceding it—we can't help but notice how previous details all seem to be pointing to this one indelible scene.

As bystanders, we hear Jesus speak openly about the plan. But the disciples just aren't grasping what's to take place. We witness Jesus willingly enter Jerusalem. Wait a second! Isn't this the place He should have avoided?

Yes! It was here that His enemies were lying in wait, looking for an opportunity to accuse Him. Yet, Jesus willingly goes. He's not forced. He simply *goes*.

Though it may seem He's headed in the wrong direction, He's actually walking on the road He created. And He's walking with determination. There is undaunted purpose in each step.

He walks with you in mind.

And today is lamb selection day. This is when devout Jewish people will select their lamb to commemorate the

Passover. They'll remember what God has done by bringing them out of Egypt. And, in this commemoration they'll anticipate what God will do in a renewed exodus when Messiah will come.

The city reverberates in religious activity. Behind the earthly curtain—in the spiritual realm—the Father is preparing *His* Lamb. This Passover will be different. And the Son is keenly aware.

This is the Passover in which God will confront His people with the question we're still answering: "Will you choose *My* Lamb?"

About 25 years later, the apostle Paul would parallel this day in his letter to the Corinthians: **"For Christ, our Passover lamb, has been sacrificed."**
(1 Corinthians 5:7 NIV)

Linda remembers the day she made her choice:

I remember one Sunday morning, more than 50 years ago when God spoke to my 9-year-old heart. During the preaching, my little heart was so convicted of sin that I knew without doubt I needed Jesus in my life.

So I rushed to the altar to pray for forgiveness. Sure, I wanted to avoid hell—but even more—I wanted to avoid being separated from God. During the service, I sensed a genuine need for Him in my life. I'll never forget when I knelt at the altar. I experienced a deep sense of His peace and joy. That moment is still a vivid memory.

As the years have passed, the desire to stay close to God has continued to grow in my life. I want to please Him, and I want to serve Him. He's done so much for me. He chose me, and I'm so glad that I had the opportunity to choose Him at an early age. Now, living in Mount Pleasant, Texas, I continue to fall in love with Him more and more each day of my life.

***

Back to Passover Day.
God was confronting His people.
And, He's still confronting today.
Jesus lived a life of love. But in exchange, He was subjected to hate. The equation—as lopsided as it was—was pronounced by most of His own people, the Jews:

Jesus + Love = Hate.

He extended acceptance and forgiveness to those He encountered. And in return? Rejection. False accusations.

Remembering the Story

As we stand amidst the crowd, we savor the memories.
His young mother.
A manger.
A patient and hard-working daddy placing a hammer in the hands of Christ, teaching him to build. Yet only a few years later, the hammer would attach those hands to a Cross for all of humanity. Still . . . He never lost His appreciation of the smell of sawdust and freshly-cut wood.
The temple—where at only age 12—He had mesmerized the religious leaders with adult wisdom.

Then later commissioning 12 ordinary men to make a career change and follow Him. They had pursued Him with reverent—yet confused—passion. Perceiving His identity when He conversed with weather . . . and it responded.

In awe as He placed mud on the eyes of a blind man then commanded him to look in His face and view genuine love.

Constant interruptions.

Jairus' plea for his daughter.

A woman with diseased blood.

A man possessed by so many demons that even Satan himself had lost count.

And the banquet! Jesus had served thousands—with only a few slices of bread and a handful of very small fish.

Lazarus.

His body embalmed and wrapped in cloths.

Buried securely in the family tomb.

Dead.

> The crowd salivates for His blood.

Yet with the same authority that fashioned humanity from a fistful of dirt, his name is called and blood courses through his veins once again. A heart surrendered to fatality, instantly revived. A corpse smothered in the stench of death . . . walking . . . out . . . of . . . the . . . tomb . . . *Lazarus.* Removing his own burial clothes.

And now, the Cross.

We're back in the present. The *now* is extremely real. We remember the journey to this moment. The road had been long. But hadn't it always been leading to this? Golgotha. The skull-shaped hill.

This is why He came. Each step has brought Him here.

The past few days, and especially the last several hours, have been incomprehensible. Betrayal.

The cat-of-nine-tails ripping apart tendons and ligaments. Again. And again. His raw flesh hanging in strips.

Illegal trials.

Fraudulent testimonies.

Orchestrated mockery.

Erroneous accusations.

The Creator judged by His creation.

But wait. Pilate is hesitant. What's he saying? There's no *cause* for His execution. Words so stunning they're cemented into Scripture. Luke 23:13-25 echoes the ruler's announcement that Jesus doesn't deserve death.

What an understatement.

As we watch the scene unfold, we know Jesus has authority *over* death. Surely, death won't call *His* name.

Yet the crowd salivates for His blood. And our hearts plummet as Barabbas enters the scene. An insurrectionist. He's a murderer. *This* is what a criminal looks like. This is a man whose life deserves death.

Oscillating emotions. Pilate seeks to bargain the release of Jesus with Barabbas. The governor has the authority to release our Savior.

Three times he negotiates.

And three times the crowd abrogates with their thirst for the most horrific of deaths: Crucifixion.

A bowl of water . . . probably from the Sea of Galilee.

Pilate absurdly washes his hands.

The water that once suspended Christ on its crest now envelops the hands of a self-absorbed, weak governor as he claims he's no longer responsible.

Jesus takes the criminal's place, and Barabbas is released.

Execution.

The juxtaposition is inescapable:

> Forgiveness hovers like an umbrella over hearts of stone.

Royalty crowned with thorns.

Creation killing the Creator.

Despite the paradox, while shouts of hate are hurled upward to the Cross—words saturated in love rain on the crowd of accusers. Forgiveness hovers like an umbrella over hearts of stone.

"Father, forgive them, for they do not know what they do." (Luke 23:34 NKJV)

Questions

As Christ-followers, we're definitely in the minority with this crowd of vile hecklers surrounding Golgotha. But with our attention fixed on three crosses, we begin to see the unimaginable. A steeled heart starts to soften.

Jesus is hanging between two criminals. One blasphemes God's Son. The other asks a question. And we remember how Jesus embraces questions.

We flash back to a woman conversing with Him at a well: "Where can I get this living water?"

And with Nicodemus late in the evening: "How can I be born again?"

With Thomas: "How can we know the way?"

And just hours earlier with Pilate: "What is truth?" as he stared Truth in the face.

And now with a thief whose death is imminent: "Will You remember me in Your kingdom?"

Our hearts warm as we see Jesus emanating love. "Yes." We think of our own questions, and how He has patiently exchanged them with solidity and faith.

The thief, with no apparent hope—his life slipping away—receives the promise from Jesus that they *will* be united in God's Kingdom.

The seemingly unredeemable, redeemed.

The enslaved, set free.

This is Our Story

As the scene unfolds, we realize that this is *our* story. Jesus has taken *our* place. Don't we all possess a bit of Barabbas identity? Haven't we, too, broken God's law? We know what it's like to head down the wrong road. We're all too familiar with misconstrued directions.

Like Linda, Emily came to that realization at a young age in Ohio:

I grew up knowing about Jesus. My parents began teaching me the Word of God at a young age. They were also faithful to model what a Christian looked like. It was easy to see their commitment to Christ in their lives. They were involved in ministry, attended church consistently and brought others to Him. Actually, my mom was the one who led me to Jesus after a series of lies I had told when I was 8 years old. I felt so guilty that I tossed and turned for several nights.

I was in the second grade and absolutely adored my teacher, Mrs. Forte. The last thing I wanted was to disappoint her. I had cheated on an assignment, because I hadn't finished my work and then lied to Mrs. Forte about it.

That night as I lay in bed, I was haunted by how many lies I'd been telling—anything from fighting with my brother to lying to my teacher. I felt so guilty that I told my mom the truth about what had happened.

The Holy Spirit convicted me of my sin until I couldn't take it anymore. I had heard others pray for forgiveness, and now it was my turn. With my mom's help, I confessed and asked Jesus into my heart that night. The guilt lifted, and I remember thinking, *Wow, Jesus is so real!*

***

When we're headed in the wrong direction, it's easy to break God's law. Each of us has known that guilt. But because Jesus has taken our place, we can turn around and go free. This becomes our story.

Before we rejoin the crowd around the Cross, let's continue with Emily for a few moments:

I wish that I could say that I lived faithfully from that time at 8 years old when I knew that Jesus was so real . . . but I can't. There seemed to be a distorted ebb and flow to my teen years. I'd get on fire for Jesus, then I'd fail Him and wander. After a while, I'd rededicate my life to Him but end up repeating the same pattern.

During my sophomore year of high school our church board hired a youth pastor. That summer I rededicated my life to Christ (again) and grew much stronger in my relationship with God. For months it seemed as though I was really on top of it spiritually.

My youth pastor genuinely cared, and I was able to open up about my spiritual inconsistency. Our youth ministry was amazing. It was spiritual and fun! My youth pastor and Christian friends became my new social group. I was growing deeper spiritually, and this was the longest amount of time I walked in victory.

But after a while, things began to unravel.

The Plummet

When I was 17, I ran into an old fling who was now in college. Mike noticed something different about me, and I told him about my relationship with Jesus. His response surprised me. "You found God? That's awesome. My family isn't religious, and I've always wanted to know more about God. You really seem happy and different."

Because Mike genuinely wanted to know more about Christ, we planned a time to meet, and I was excited to share my faith with him. I explained that I'd be bringing a few other Christians with me, because I wanted him to know this wasn't a date. He restated that he really desired to know about God.

The night before we were going to meet, he was tragically killed while driving drunk. I was devastated. It didn't make sense. I was going to share Jesus with him. I was hoping he would become a Christian. But now the opportunity was gone. I was confused and angry. And I sensed a pervasive aura of darkness around me.

After the funeral, I converged my rage into one thought: *God, why didn't You stop this so my friend could have been saved?*

In my confusion I began to search for answers. I resorted to my old life, old friends and old ways. One night I really needed some answers, so I went to my best friend's house. She wasn't home, so I drove to my youth pastor's.

When I arrived, he was home alone; his wife and child were away. When he invited me in, I knew I shouldn't be alone with a married man. But I went inside.

His comforting words turned into temptation. He told me how much he cared about me. I realized it was an inappropriate conversation; it was way more than pastoral. I knew it was wrong. But I was so vulnerable after the death of my friend.

His words led to action, and I found myself in his arms. I needed to run, but I didn't. And, even though we didn't have sex—I still knew it was adulterous. My respect for him quickly turned to hate. I was afraid this affair would be exposed, and my fear led me deeper into the things of the world. Our involvement continued for a short while until he moved out of town.

After he moved, he called and tried to convince me to move with him when I turned 18. I hung up on him. He left ministry, and I wanted to hide. I was steeped in defeat.

This is the condition I was in when I left home to attend a Christian college. I really wanted to change but I couldn't shake the shame, self-hatred, anger and guilt. I hated life. I detested my family, and I despised that man who ruined me. How could I have allowed this to happen? I no longer respected myself. If I could have gone back in time, I would have made completely different choices.

But I couldn't. So I hated myself.

***

Time Suspended

Self-hatred is often a by-product of going the wrong direction. And as we stand with the angry mob at Golgotha, we wonder what happened in these people's lives to set them in the wrong direction. The cursing flows so easily. The anger directed toward a loving Savior seems abnormally natural with them.

We shift our weight and continue to glance through the crowd.

How much time has passed since we saw Jesus—almost beyond human recognition—stumble with the load of His Cross? We watched as Simon of Cyrene shouldered the instrument of death on his own arms and carried it the remaining distance to the skull-shaped hill.

> Self-hatred is often a by-product of going the wrong direction.

But we have lost track of time.

Has it been hours?

A full day?

It seems time and weather and atmosphere have become pendulous.

We rejoice with the thief's dramatic realization that even on a cross, Divinity offers redemption. God has literally invaded his life with love. This thief encountered a fatal roadblock, but Jesus gave him new direction.

Forgiveness.

Transformation.

We're familiar with roadblocks. It's how we react to them that determines change—for the good or the bad. Let's find out how Emily responded to her roadblock.

I had just started college, and I was alone in my dorm room. My past haunted me. I was obsessed with a paralyzing fear that people would find out about my involvement with our former youth pastor. Then what would I do? How would my friends at this Christian college respond? How would the people in my church react? What would my family say?

I was tired of living like this, but the lies replayed themselves over and over in my mind. I lived in a state of panic. And that night, alone in my room, a demonic presence filled the air.

I couldn't see it, but I was keenly aware of it. *I felt it.* Demonic thoughts swirled inside my head—hideous thoughts that I'd never considered before. I have never felt so defenselessly frightened in my life. The presence told me to end it. The overwhelming thought, *Just kill yourself*, had taken my mind captive.

And in that moment of desperation—I knew I had to make a decision. Would I go ahead and end it all? Or would I live? I realized heaven and hell were battling for my soul, and I had the authority to cast the deciding vote.

"Jesus! Help me!"

"Jesus! Help me!"

"Jesus! Help me!" I shouted it again and again. Over and over. I fell to the floor on my face, crying out for Jesus to take all of me. I couldn't live another moment without Him. "Forgive me, Father. Save me. Heal me. Deliver me."

I continued to pray.

As I did, the demonic oppression that I was experiencing left the room and was replaced by the sweet presence of the Holy Spirit. Waves of grace flowed over my body and through my entire being in such a tangible way as Jesus healed me.

Through hours of Jesus revealing and tearing down barriers I'd built, I knew my past was finally in the past. And, with Him, my future was without limit. Tomorrow would be a new day!

***

Tomorrow

Oh, how we yearn for a new day! We weep as we watch Christ struggle to inhale. And though His last words are labored, there's no mistaking His conversation with the Giver of Life: "Father, into your hands I commend My Spirit."

The sky darkens.

Earth trembles.

The curtain inside the temple is torn from top to bottom. The holy of holies is no longer separated from mankind. Through His death, we now have access to Father God. Tomorrow *will* come.

Three days later we rejoice in exultation as our Savior lives. He *does* have authority over death. He resurrects Himself. He lives. And we have tomorrow, today.

> We no longer have to remain paralyzed by fatal roadblocks.

We no longer have to remain paralyzed by fatal roadblocks. He forgives. And He even chooses to forget.

Psalm 103:12 reminds us that our sins have been removed **"as far as the east is from the west."** If you go east, you'll never find yourself going west.

Micah 7:19 assures us that He hurls our sins into the depths of the sea. How deep is that sea? It doesn't matter. No need to go diving. It's time to move on. This is the moment for divine redirection. That's what the thief received. And that's what Emily accepted. Here's the rest of her story:

It's amazing what brokenness can lead to. Crying out to God and being filled with the Holy Spirit brings new life. By giving all the pain of my past to Him, the deepest wounds of my soul were healed. My mind and heart experienced love, joy and peace.

After Jesus turned me around, I discovered what life was truly about. The lies of the enemy only led me to defeat. But Jesus redirected me to abundant life! He came through in my darkest hour.

For 20 years I've lived in freedom from the darkness I once experienced. I'm living proof of what Christ can do for a condemned, hopeless soul who surrenders to His will. I'm a new creation, I'm never going back.

***

Our Invitation

Can you identify with the thief? Maybe you feel you've hit a fatal roadblock. And perhaps, like Emily once did, you've started believing the lies of the enemy.

The transformed thief's story is *our* story. The Divine has taken our place. We can make a decision today to turn around, to be redirected by Him.

The reality is this: It's never too late to turn around. Never. Never. Never. EVER.

Our Savior is quick to save, forgive and to divinely redirect.

But we have a responsibility with the redemption that Jesus gives. Sometimes this new path will require us to repair things harmed along the way.

The thief didn't have the opportunity to do this. But we do. When we realize we don't live life in seclusion, it should cause us to understand our responsibility to those around us. There are other travelers on the road we may have hurt along the way.

Although it's impossible to go back in time and make different choices, restitution *can* be made and healing can come. The Hebrew writer (12:14) instructs us to spare no effort to live at peace with all men in order to achieve holiness. With all the determination of a skilled athlete we must pursue this path.

Jesus talks about the responsibility to reconcile any wrong with our fellow man (see Matthew 5:23). So, part of our turnaround must be recognition of this responsibility. Effort can be made to restore broken relationships. Forgiveness must be sought. Wrongs can be righted. It's a new way of living. That's what redirection is all about. This is the redirection that only Jesus can give.

And oh, how sweet that redirection can be! Need proof? After you've finished the study section on page 192, we'll join our friends again on the road to Emmaus. It may surprise you what they discover during an evening snack.

Chapter Eleven
Redirection Becomes Sweet

We're back on the road with the two disciples on their way to Emmaus. When we left them in chapter four, Jesus had caught up with them and listened intently as they shared partial truths about what had happened. Remember, they haven't recognized Jesus.

They're on the right road, but they're headed in the wrong direction. They were told to wait in Jerusalem, but they walked the opposite way. They're living in total defeat, and their broken dreams are clouding their spiritual vision.

Maybe you can relate. Hannah certainly can.

About 3 years ago—at the age of 22—I was diagnosed with a rare inflammatory muscle disease called polymyositis. Up to that, I had been fortunate to enjoy perfect health, so this diagnosis definitely rocked my world.

One day I was healthy, and the next day I could barely walk. Every muscle ached. Because of this, I had numerous accidents. I'd fall and have to go to the E.R. to make sure I didn't break any bones or get a concussion.

It took months for my doctors to diagnose my disease. I was tested for lupus, fibromyalgia, multiple sclerosis and cancer. I was thankful that it wasn't any of those, but I was still terrified with the word *disease* that the physicians were using with me.

I've been a believer from a very young age, and I was reared in a strong Christian home. So my first reaction, even though I was terrified, was to trust that God was in control. However, as the weeks and months went on, and my doctors couldn't get my disease under control, I became angry at God.

My prayers turned into shouting matches aimed at heaven. Through tears I prayed, "God, if You're so powerful, why haven't You healed me?"

He never answered.

But He *did* give me comfort through family members and friends who were praying for me. In those dark moments, I found myself crawling with hope in His power of healing.

Living in Defeat

My hope didn't last long. Several months ago, I found myself in the lowest, darkest season of my life. I'd been receiving treatment at the end of 2017 that had been making huge improvements to my symptoms. I felt strong again.

But in January 2018, my insurance company decided to stop covering these expensive treatments. This left me with no choice but to discontinue the infusions until further notice. It was six months of constant back-and-forth negotiating with my insurance company, begging them to let me have the treatments. And in that process, I lost hope. I didn't see God working on my behalf, my health was starting to decline again, and I didn't see the point in fighting for quality of life anymore.

I was living in such defeat; I was unable to see or feel God's presence any longer. My desperation turned into depression. I truly couldn't see any end in sight. I empathize with those who feel there's no hope and consider taking their own lives.

The darkness continued to consume me, and I shut myself off from feelings and turned into a robot. If I allowed myself to feel, I'd have to face the fear. I hit rock bottom.

What Now?

Fortunately, instead of allowing me to stay at the bottom of my pit, God rescued me. Through the Holy Spirit, He convicted me of my attitude of worry and replaced it with joy. And He replaced my anxiety with His peace.

I didn't see Him for so long because I actively shut Him out. I was so defeated, I *couldn't* see Him in my life or even feel His presence. I realize now, though, that He was always there—just waiting to be known again.

My prayer in sharing my story is that others will know of God's faithfulness. Even in our darkest moments, even when we turn away from Him, and even when we choose to live in defeat, He's waiting for us to recognize Him.

And even in the midst of physical pain, broken dreams, and emotional heartbreak, His peace is everlasting. No, I don't suddenly have it all together. But I'm living each day at a time through God's perfect grace and no longer living in defeat.

***

The Disciples Dish It Out

Jesus listens to the disciples unload—even though they're only buying into partial truths of what has happened. They haven't said anything that's false. The only problem is, it's not the *whole* truth.

We can't simply take part of the truth and believe only what we want to believe. If we're going to buy into the Truth, we have to buy into the *whole* Truth and nothing but the Truth. Not doing so is exactly how bad doctrine develops. One little group over here grabs a little section of Scripture and interprets the whole Bible that way.

> They're on the right road, but they're headed in the wrong direction.

No. Truth doesn't work that way. The Bible is all one book. We can't simply pick and choose which parts we accept. We have a responsibility to God and others to correctly handle His Word. These two disciples didn't, and it brought them to despair.

We could say these two disciples had all the pieces of the puzzle; they just failed to put it together. The faith of these two men was tied to the things that they'd seen—not to what Jesus had said. And Jesus wants to move them from physical sight to spiritual sight.

Whaaaat?

Jesus never misses an exit. It wasn't an accident that He's with these two men. He purposely showed up at exactly the right time. He allows the two men to empty their hearts, then without hesitation, our Savior catapults right inside of His own prophecies.

Jesus lets them have it!

This is where the story gets really good.

Fasten your seatbelts.

We're picking up the speed!

"He said to them, 'How foolish you are, and how slow to believe all that the prophets have spoken!'" (Luke 24:25 NIV)

Jesus comes on pretty strong here, doesn't He? "How foolish you are!" In the King James Version it reads, **"Oh, fools!"**

Jesus never spoke flippantly.

He chose His words carefully.

There are very few times in Scripture that we hear Him say "fools."

These two disciples knew the Word. They knew what it meant to be called a fool. Let's look at what the Old Testament says about a fool:

"The fool says in his heart, 'There is no God.'" (Psalm 13:1 NIV)

So by calling them fools, they knew exactly what He was saying. They knew the meaning of a fool. And so Jesus is saying, "By your actions, you're living as though there is no God. There's no one in control. You fools...."

We Can Relate

Sometimes we find ourselves living the same way—
   an election doesn't turn out how we want.
      We disagree with a law that's passed.
         We act as though no one's in control.
           God is STILL on the throne!
              He's still in control.

He sometimes chooses to work behind the scenes . . . but He's still on the throne.

What does Jesus do next?

He begins with Moses and going through all the prophets, He expounds on what Scripture says about Himself. Jesus is explaining the prophecies given about Him.

Wow.

What a message.

Jesus is actually preaching to these two men.

And He's a good preacher.

Why?

Because He's preaching the Word.

This is one reason why we can't ignore the Old Testament. A lot of people say it's irrelevant—that we should just focus on the New Testament. But the Old Testament is about Jesus. And Jesus reveals Himself through the Old Testament prophets.

Think about what's happening here.

(This is good stuff!)

We see the *resurrected Word*

revealing the *living* Word

through the *written Word.*

We have the fulfillment explaining the prophecy!

Awesome!

In fact, it's so thrilling, we need to read it again:

We see the *resurrected Word*

revealing the *living* Word

through the *written Word.*

We have the fulfillment explaining the prophecy!

Nowhere else could this happen except with Christ and the Bible.

The fulfillment is explaining the prophecy.

It all points to Him.

As we continue walking with these two men, we notice a transition that begins to occur as Jesus reveals Himself through the Word. Before . . . their hearts were overwhelmed with the sadness and with their circumstances, but now as Jesus begins to teach, their minds have been opened to the Savior as He's revealed in Scripture.

The Arrival

Our GPS now reveals where we are. The disciples arrive at their destination. They've reached Emmaus. And there was something about their traveling Companion that has struck a chord deep within their hearts. They still don't recognize Him as Christ, but they want to spend more time with Him.

Jesus starts to move on without them, but Cleopas and his friend ask Him to stay for a while longer. "The day is over. No need to keep walking in the dark."

> There has to come a time when Jesus becomes the Host.

"That's right. Come on in. You can stay here tonight. Let's share a meal and talk some more."

Jesus always goes where He's invited.

Bonnie and her husband love having their three adult sons home for holidays. "Two of our boys live here in the same state as we do, but our middle son, Lee, lives on the East Coast," she says. "Holidays have always been a special family time—especially Christmas. We love to read the Christmas story from Luke, spend time in prayer and just enjoy one another's company as we share gifts.

When Lee was in college near Boston, Bonnie realized she and her husband didn't have the money to fly him home for Christmas. "Even though I had spent the morning searching online for an airline ticket, the prices were extremely high, and my heart sank when I realized it was out of our control. How could we enjoy Christmas without all three boys here with us?"

She also knew his campus would close for the holidays. Though he could remain in his dorm, he'd be without food unless he braved the bitter cold and walked a few miles to the nearest restaurant.

"I immediately invited Jesus into the situation," Bonnie says. "God has always been the center of our home, and my husband prays on his knees every night before climbing into bed. We've seen God do more for us than I could ever explain."

After praying about the matter, Bonnie was suddenly overwhelmed with a deep peace. "I knew immediately it was the Lord," she says. "He seemed to say, 'Trust Me. You've invited Me to take over, so just trust Me."

Bonnie continued her workday with a lightened heart and increased faith. "I actually stopped thinking and worrying about it," she says.

When she got home after work, she noticed the message light blinking on their answering machine. "I wept as I listened to the message from a dear friend," Bonnie says.

"Hey, Bonnie. It's Shelley. I'm flying from Chicago to Cincinnati today, and my Chicago flight is full. They asked for volunteers to take a later flight. For some reason, Lee popped into my mind. I don't know if you've already purchased an airline ticket for him to come home for Christmas, but by waiting here a few more hours in Chicago and taking a later flight, I'm getting a voucher good for a round-trip ticket anywhere in the States. I'll send it to you to make sure Lee gets home for Christmas. Love you!"

"I believed it, but I couldn't believe it," Bonnie says. "Yes, I had invited Jesus into this seemingly impossible situation. And yes, I believed He could take care of it. But I had no idea it would come this quickly or be this easy. And I knew Shelley loved to travel. She could have easily used that voucher on a vacation for herself. But God was moving! He worked in *my* life to remind me that He always shows up where He's invited, and that He cares about our family being together. And He also moved in Shelley's life to bring my son to her mind."

When Bonnie and her husband met Lee at the airport, he was running a fever and had a severe case of strep throat. "We went straight from the airport to the emergency room," she says "He spent the entire Christmas break in bed recuperating, but I had the privilege of caring for him as only a mother can.

"I shudder to think of the possibility of him being alone in a big dorm without medicine, running a fever, no access to a nurse, no car. God is certainly in the business of caring for His children."

Lee needed to be home that Christmas—maybe just to get well—and God made sure it happened.

***

Jesus goes where He's invited.

So He enters the house with Cleopas and his friend, and we see them sitting at the table. Jesus is the invited guest, but the custom of the time is being ignored because Jesus begins playing the role of host.

Have you ever wondered why some of us never know His power? We invite Him in, but we want to stay in control. Yes, we welcome Him inside, but we want to play our own roles—the roles we've chosen for ourselves.

There has to come a time when Jesus becomes the Host.

The One in charge.

It makes sense that if you want to know Him in His fullness—if you want to live in His power—He *must* be the honored Host in your life.

Wait a second! How do we know Jesus took the role of host once He stepped inside the house with these two disciples?

> Jesus passionately desires to divinely redirect your steps with hope.

Because while the three of them are sitting at the table, Jesus picks up the bread, breaks it and hands it to the disciples. That's not the job of a guest.

And if we research the Greek language in which the New Testament was originally written, we see that the grammatical tense used here literally means the two men take the bread from His hands. It's not that He's simply giving—they *take* the bread from His hands.

This is exactly what Jesus wants us to do.

He wants us to take what He offers us.

Recap

Let's do a quick recap of what's happening here at the table.

Jesus assumes the role of Host.
He picks up the bread.
He breaks the bread.
He offers it, and these two disciples take the bread.
And when they take the bread, their eyes are opened.
Let this soak in, because it's a powerful picture.
They were discouraged.
Their minds were opened by the Teacher.
Their hearts were stirred.
And as they took the bread, NOW they could see.
It deserves repeating:
When they took the bread NOW they could see.
Undeniable truth.
Now they recognize Him. Now they see Jesus.
It's Him!
It's the Son of God who's sitting with them.
It's the Messiah who's been walking with them, teaching them.
This is the One who had hung on the tree.
He was alive. He IS alive!
Why? How did they suddenly recognize Him?

Could they have been part of the 5,000 the day they saw these same hands multiply bread and fish to feed the hungry multitude? Maybe. But unless they were standing right next to Him, it would have been difficult to see His hands in a crowd that large.

More than likely, it's because they saw His wounds. When Jesus picked up the bread and held it out to them, they would have *had* to see His wounds from just three days ago. They saw the wounds the nails had left. And when they saw those wounds—when their eyes were opened— He disappeared.

Let's get back to Scripture:

"When he was at the table with them, he took bread, gave thanks, broke it and began to give it to them. Then their eyes were opened and they recognized him, and he disappeared from their sight.

"They asked each other, 'Were not our hearts burning within us while he talked with us on the road and opened the Scriptures to us?' " (Luke 24:30-32 NIV)

This is what happens when we see the Living Word coming out of the Written Word! Our hearts are moved. We can't help but be stirred.

What happened next?

"They got up and returned at once to Jerusalem. There they found the Eleven and those with them, assembled together." (Luke 24:33 NIV)

Right Road, Right Direction

These two men are mentally exhausted. They're physically drained. They've just walked seven miles in the blazing heat. The sun has set. The day is over.

But now we see them filled with excitement and energy. They *were* discouraged. Now they're *encouraged*. They're full of hope! Why? Because they'd spent time with Jesus Himself.

This is what happens with us as well. Think of a time when you were at the end of your rope. Once you got into the Written Word and spent time with the Living Word, the Resurrected Word resurrects YOU!

I, too, have been resurrected by the Living Word through the Written Word. When my dad passed away two years ago, I clung to God's promises. Because my mom had died 14 years ago, I felt like an orphan when I lost Dad.

I've never been married, so I didn't have a husband to lean on, but by saturating myself in the Bible, I truly felt God lifting my sadness through His holy Word:

"For your Maker is your husband—the Lord Almighty is his name." (Isaiah 54:5 NIV)

"When you go through deep waters and great trouble, I will be with you. When you go through rivers of difficulty, you will not drown! When you walk through the fire of oppression, you will not be burned up—the flames will not consume you."
(Isaiah 43:2 LB)

"The Lord is close to the brokenhearted and saves those who are crushed in spirit." (Psalm 34:18 NIV)

"Blessed are those who mourn, for they will be comforted." (Matthew 5:4 NIV)

Though I was grieving, I was genuinely being comforted by the Living Word through the Written Word as the Resurrected Word resurrected *me!* I was acutely aware of His presence, and it was so very, very sweet. I clung to His promises. —**Susie**

***

Cleopas and his friend ran to where the 11 disciples were meeting and told them what had happened. Let's keep moving through this exciting drama:

"While they were still talking about this, Jesus himself stood among them and said to them, 'Peace be with you.'
"They were startled and frightened, thinking they saw a ghost. He said to them, 'Why are you troubled, and why do doubts rise in your minds?
" 'Look at my hands and my feet. It is I myself! Touch me and see; a ghost does not have flesh and bones, as you see I have.'
"When he had said this, he showed them his hands and feet." (Luke 34:36-40 NIV)

Are you so close to Jesus that you're seeing His hands? Are you watching His hands work in your life? Can you see His hands actively involved in our world?

If not . . . maybe it's because you've never truly allowed Him to become your host.

If you yearn to see His hand moving in your life, but you don't . . . maybe it's because you're not in the Word.

Could it be that you don't really know the Resurrected Word through the Living Word as revealed in the Written Word?

Here's the pattern: When you see Him and your mind is opened, your heart is stirred and He has control. His hand is revealed in your life.

It's powerful.

So powerful, it can wreck you.

In a really, really, really good way.

Here's the bottom line:

For the Christian, hope is available in a hopeless world.

For the child of God, hope is found in what God has *said* not in what we *see*.

Will you read that aloud?

True hope for the child of God is found in what God has said—not in what we see.

Two defeated men were on the right road but heading in the wrong direction. But after encountering the living Christ they suddenly turned around. After Jesus disappeared, they got up and ran to Jerusalem.

This is amazing, because remember what they'd said to Jesus?

"The day is over. Stay here." But now—suddenly in the midst of darkness—light shines through.

They have a story to tell. There's something that's burning in their hearts so much that though they dragged their feet to Emmaus, they're now racing to Jerusalem.

They're headed in the right direction. They have allowed Him to divinely redirect their lives. And guess what they were shouting: "He's alive! He's alive! He's alive!"

It changed them.

What About Us?

Some of us need to see His hands.

Some of us have been consumed with the wrong things.

We've failed to place the highest priority where it *should* be.

Victory has been bought.

Mercy has been given.

The price has been paid.

Do you see Him? Do you recognize Him? Let's get our eyes off of the things of the world. Let's stop being preoccupied with that junk. He wants to lead us out of it. We are in the world but not of the world. We need to get our eyes on what we should have them on—Jesus Christ!

If you'll learn to focus on Him through His Word, you'll see His hands. Let this truth grab you. Let this truth transform you.

When people get on our nerves, what does it teach us?

It shows us we need to be in the Word more.

When we're discouraged and walking in defeat, what we can learn?

We discover that we need to be in the Word more.

When we're on the right road but find ourselves heading the wrong direction, what is God telling us?

He's revealing that we need to be in the Word more.

It always points back to this.

We often pray, "God do something!" He *is* doing something. And we need to get right in the middle of what He's doing, but we can't until we're centered in His Word.

Focus on what He's saying. Latch onto His Word. Buy into it.

Be transformed. We have a story to tell.

Two men whom Jesus pursued had lost hope. They were consumed with things they had seen. They were experiencing extreme disappointment. But Jesus points to Himself through His Word, and through His Word they were made aware of His hands—revealing His identity.

The Final Scene

And now we come to the final scene. It's you and me. Jesus is pursuing us. Does this give you hope? Perhaps you've been staring at the darkness and need to see His light piercing through the gloom. Maybe you've hit a roadblock, come to a dead-end or taken the wrong exit.

The good news is that Jesus passionately desires to divinely redirect your steps with hope and renewed purpose and unwavering faith. As you walk in this way, He longs to reveal Himself to a world that needs to know this hope through you. When we begin to spend more and more time with Jesus, our lives will become a loud proclamation:

He's alive!

Now that the disciples are on the right road and heading the right direction, can they maintain *consistency* in the right direction? Isn't that the question we all want answered?

Go ahead and complete the study section on page 193, then we'll look at the key to maintaining the right direction and consistent spiritual growth. Yes, that CAN be ours!

Chapter Twelve
Redirection Is a Wonderful Thing

Have you ever found yourself longing for the spiritual "good ol' days"? Remember how excited you were when you first invited Jesus into your life and began a relationship with Him?

You were overcome with gratitude with His mercy that granted forgiveness for sins. You were blown away by the fact He chose to wipe your slate completely clean and even decided to *forget* your sins:

"I will forgive their wickedness and will remember their sins no more." (Jeremiah 31:34 NIV)

You couldn't wait to read your Bible each day.
You had an active prayer life.
You loved talking about Jesus.
But after a while, something happened.
Maybe you became a little lax in your daily time with Him. Church didn't seem as important. The distractions of daily life crowded into your routine and took control.
Oh, you still love Jesus.
And you're still walking with Him. It's just that things have waned a bit. The thirst for spiritual growth that once filled your life isn't as strong anymore. We *could* say . . . you've lost your cutting edge.

That sharp, spiritual cutting edge you used to have seems to be a good memory but no longer a current reality.

Mikayla from Houston, Minn., knows what that's like.

I was 21, and though I had been spiritually on fire in the past, my excitement for God somehow became stale, and my church attendance was sporadic. But when I *did* attend, I was welcomed by a 40-year-old lady named Teresa. She was a lovely woman who consistently reached out to me.

One Sunday morning, she was handing out church newsletters in the lobby. Each letter had the name of a family on it so everyone would be aware of updates, activities and needs in the church. I asked her to flip through the stack and see if my name was on one of them. She couldn't find one for me but gave me one anyway. (I later discovered I was included under my family's name).

I jokingly said, "You know these letters would look so much more interesting if you'd add a cute picture of an elephant or another fun animal on the outside."

The next week, I received a newsletter in a beautiful envelope with the most adorable little elephant on it.

Fast Forward

Just a few months later, she and her husband were in a tragic car accident that led to their passing shortly afterward. It was then that I had an "ah-ha" moment. God spoke to me and reminded me of His reality and the fact that He is constantly watching over me. I was immediately drawn once again into His love. I have my spiritual cutting edge back. I'm on fire for Jesus! I love sharing Him with others and talking about my faith.

I know Teresa is with her Creator. I was told that the morning of the accident, she had been reading the Bible—as she did each day—and the passage she was absorbing was 2 Corinthians 4:7-9. This has now become my favorite. Here it is:

"But this precious treasure—this light and power that now shine within us—is held in a perishable container, that is, in our weak bodies. Everyone can see that the glorious power within must be from God and is not our own.

"We are pressed on every side by troubles, but not crushed and broken. We are perplexed because we don't know why things happen as they do, but we don't give up and quit. We are hunted down, but God never abandons us. We get knocked down, but we get up again and keep going." (LB)

I'm so grateful that God guided me back to the dedicated relationship I had with Him in the past. It's wonderful to be spiritually alert and on fire again!

Good News

We *can* get redirected. It's possible to get that spiritual cutting edge back again. But sometimes God will allow us to go through a painful season to get our attention and help us regain our spiritual cutting edge. Trisha from Montpelier, Ind., can relate.

About 15 years ago I was praying for a new job as well as salvation for my extended family. I had always asked

God to do whatever it would take to keep me in the center of His will.

One Saturday morning I woke up and looked in the mirror. Each morning I began my day with this prayer: "Lord, You have my life, my job, my family."

But this particular morning, I didn't have it in me. I had become discouraged because I wasn't seeing answers to my prayers. Very quietly, in my spirit, I said, "I'm done. I can't do this anymore. I can't continue to pray and expect answers when I'm clearly not getting any. I still love You, God, but I'm really tired of this."

This was January, and the weather in Indiana was nasty. I climbed into my two-week-old car and headed for work. I was almost halfway there when I encountered a large truck sliding into my lane. I swerved to avoid wrecking—and in doing so—I flipped three-and-a-half times. I remember screaming, "Oh, God, help me!" as I turned in what seemed like slow motion.

My new car was now a smashed lunchbox. God definitely had my attention. Every window was broken except the one where I was. Every door was unable to be opened except the one on the driver's side.

I was walked out of the car thinking it was my spirit that was leaving the wreck, and I'd turn around and see my dead body in the driver's seat. I looked at my hands and noticed one broken fingernail. I looked in the mirror and saw two small scratches on my face.

God spoke to me: "Trisha, I love you. Trust Me. You're not finished. Let's get those hands back into service for Me."

I definitely got my spiritual cutting edge back, and I'm now a pastor's wife with two children and loving my involvement in ministry. God gently redirected me when I had decided to take a side road in my faith."

***

Getting Redirected

Getting that spiritual cutting-edge back isn't as difficult as you may think. In fact, Scripture actually gives us exact guidance on *how* to get back to where we once were spiritually.

Let's take the next exit and enter Ephesus in AD 96. We'll meet an entire group of people who have lost their spiritual cutting edge. As we enter Ephesus, you'll notice it's located on the Aegean Sea at the mouth of the Cayster River. Ephesus was one of the greatest seaports in the ancient world. It was known as the highway to Rome.

> Ephesus was steeped in the occult.

Because of the connection with the sea and river, Ephesus was a hubbub of travel and commerce. The Temple of Artemis was located here and was considered one of the seven wonders of the ancient world. It was huge—425 feet long, 220 feet wide and 60 feet high, and it was dedicated to the goddess of the hunt. Ephesus was a large city—it boasted a population of 300,000. But it was also a city steeped in the occult with sorcerers, witches, astrologers and wizards.

Living in the midst of this made it extremely difficult for Christians to stay pointed in the right direction. And many of them had lost their spiritual cutting edge. In fact, the church received a letter from the apostle John (written from the Island of Patmos) in which the Holy Spirit prompted him to bring the matter to their attention. Let's take a look:

"But I have something against you, that you have abandoned the love you had at first."
(Revelation 2:4 MEV)

These Christians no longer had the spiritual cutting edge they once had. They had been excited about living for Christ. Their lives reflected their love and commitment to Him. But the influences of wicked surroundings had influenced them in such a way that their love for Christ wasn't being evidenced as it had been.

Sound familiar?

We, too, live in a wicked world.

It's easy for us to be influenced by our surroundings.

Could the Holy Spirit be asking us the same question today? "What happened? You're not loving Me like you once did. You've lost your spiritual cutting edge."

Perhaps you took a wrong exit.

Or you made a turn that led you in the opposite direction of where you should have gone. Any number of things can contribute to losing our spiritual cutting edge, but something that can keep us on track is reading the Bible consistently.

I admit it.

Sometimes the Bible is just tough for me to digest—especially when I'm plodding through Leviticus. But I keep reading God's Word because I know I need it. I gain a lot of my spiritual strength from the Bible. I love the stories of ordinary people who were used by God in mighty ways.

That definitely encourages me! And the more I read His Word, the more I keep falling in love with it.

But I don't want it to become stale or routine. So I toss a few variations into my Bible reading. One year I read the entire Bible on my knees. What a glorious experience that was. Another year I read it out loud.

I also vary the translation of Bible I read each year. For example, last year I read the Modern English Version, and this year I'm reading through the New International Version. I have several different translations of the Bible, and by rotating them from year to year, I always gain fresh insight from my time in the Word. This helps keep my spiritual edge sharp and focused. —**Susie**

***

We Can Go Back

Fortunately, we don't have to remain in the neutral zone longing for the spiritual cutting edge we once had. It *is* possible to get our spiritual cutting edge back. We get specific directions from an obscure little story tucked away in the Old Testament book of 2 Kings 6:1-7.

Here's the scene: The prophet Elisha was leading a group of prophets. Think of him as their seminary president. Their meeting place had become too small and crowded. One of the students (prophets) asked Elisha if they could build a new meeting place—a new seminary—by the Jordan River.

Elisha gave permission and went with them as they began their work. One student was overly zealous. He was like a cartoon character whose motion was blurred because he was working so fast and furious. In fact, his labor was so intense, that as he was chopping down a tree, the head of his axe flew off the handle and went soaring into the Jordan.

He could have done what you and I may be tempted to do. He could have simply continued swinging the handle and beating the tree with it. *Maybe no one will notice nothing effective is happening. If I just keep going through the motions, it will look like I'm working hard for this new seminary to be built.*

> Any number of things can contribute to losing our spiritual cutting edge.

We're tempted in the same way: *If I can keep up the appearance of working hard for Jesus, maybe no one will notice there's no fruit in my life. I'll keep leading this small group, continue to attend church, keep going to Bible study . . .*

Fortunately, he didn't do that. He did what God wants all of us to do when we've lost our spiritual cutting edge. And the rest of the story in 2 Kings 6:1-7, gives us three Rs for redirecting ourselves to get back our spiritual cutting edge.

First R: Repent

"Master! I've lost it. I've lost my cutting edge." Instead of merely keeping up a good spiritual appearance, he repented. He confessed. He admitted what had happened.

We need to be honest about where we are in our relationship with Christ. If we've lost our direction, if we need re-direction or if we're walking in the opposite direction, let's admit it and get help. It's comforting to know that we can go to our Master and be honest with Him.

Elisha gave this young prophet some great advice. And that brings us to the next R.

Second R: Remember
"The man of God asked, 'Where did it fall?' "
(2 Kings 6:6 NIV)

Elisha directed the student to remember. *Where did I last have my cutting edge? Where was I? What specifically was I doing?*

Let's see. I was in that apple orchard over there. I was on the third row, fourth tree from the end of the line. Yes, that's where I was. That was the tree I was chopping on when I lost my cutting edge.

Remember.

That's solid advice.

The memory can be an amazing thing.

> We need to be honest about where we are in our relationship with Christ.

It can take us right back to where we need to be.

So where were you when you *did* have your spiritual cutting edge? What were you doing?

Well, let me think. Um, I was involved in a Bible study. Good. *And instead of listening to music in the car on my way to work, I used that time to pray.* Wonderful. *And I had accountability in my life. I was also more involved in church and ministry. I read my Bible consistently.* Those are good and very specific memories.

What did Elisha direct the prophet to do next?

Third R: Return

Once he remembered what he was doing and where he last had his cutting edge, he returned to the place where he had lost it. Elisha cut a stick and threw it in the Jordan River. The ax head miraculously floated to the surface.

" 'Lift it out,' he said. Then the man reached out his hand and took it." (2 Kings 6:6-7 NIV)

You, too, can return.
Go back to consistently reading your Bible.
Reactivate your prayer life.
Re-establish accountability in your life.
You *can* go back to where you once were spiritually.
You can once again have a spiritual cutting edge in your life.

Maintaining your Cutting Edge
Once we regain our spiritual edge, what can we do to keep it? Grace Merrill accepted Christ as her personal Savior when she was 8 years old. She recently turned 75. From Colorado Springs, Colo., she shares what helps her maintain her consistent spiritual cutting edge:

If my daily devotions begin to feel a little stale, I switch things up! I'll read out of a different Bible translation, or I'll add on a unique devotional book with my Bible reading. Sometimes I'll read the words of a hymn after my Bible reading, and some years I choose to read the One-Year Bible.

As I switch things up, I change from sequential reading to topical reading using a concordance. For example, what's everything I can find that the Bible have to say about peace? About money? About healing? Or I switch to something biographical. For instance, I'll read every reference about Barnabas, the "son of encouragement."

After I've done these things and have kept a list of what I learned, I return to sequential reading in the Bible.

Another thing that helps me maintain my excitement during my daily quite time in this: One morning a week, I re-copy my sermon notes from last Sunday into my journal. This helps that truth get more firmly cemented into my spirit, re-looking up and 'chewing on' the Scriptures.

In that same journal of sermon notes, I turn it over and keep monthly praise and prayers in the back, working forward. When the two things meet in the middle, it's time for a new book!

I've discovered that just a little creative change every now and then can make a big difference.

***

Go Ahead

Sometimes our GPS fails. There are days we all need to pull over and ask for directions. Never hesitate to do that! Your heavenly Father loves to redirect, re-establish and reactivate. It's okay . . . and even wise to ask for directions.

Complete the study section on page 195.

Individual and Small Group Study Guide

Whether you're reading this book alone or using it in a small group study, taking time to answer the questions included will help you process on a deeper level the message from each chapter.

We encourage you to actually jot your answers in the space provided. Why? Because actually writing something down, forces you to think through your response with more clarity.

Chapter One
Redirection from the Routine

Talk About It

• When you find yourself gravitating to the routine, what does that looks like for you? (For Susie, it was cleaning.)

• What measures can be taken to ensure that your routine doesn't get in the way of your becoming all God wants.

• Describe a time you did what was right even though you had no desire to do so. What were the results?

• Identify a specific time when routine hindered you from accomplishing something God wanted you to do.

• If Rachel hadn't allowed God to keep interrupting her routine, she would have never experienced the adventurous life she's now living. Can you think of a time you allowed God to break your routine to follow Him on a deeper level as Rachel did?

Pray About It

Ask God to help you obey Him—even when your flesh desires the opposite. If this is difficult for you, ask Him to help you *want* to want to follow Him in every area of your life. Invite Him to interrupt your routine.

Chapter Two
Redirection from Defeat

Talk About It

• Describe something you quit as a child but wish you hadn't. (Piano lessons, newspaper route, a specific sport, etc.)

• When are you most tempted to quit something?

• Describe the last thing you quit.

• Can you identify a time in your life when—like Chris—you were at the end of your finances and needed God to intervene?

• How does defeat influence your decision to quit or keep going?

• Have you ever felt like Elijah? Discuss a time of defeat and how God eventually gave you victory.

Pray About It

Thank God for understanding how you feel and never negating your emotions. Thank Him for knowing exactly what you need. In faith, thank Him ahead of time for providing.

Chapter Three
Redirection from Melancholy Music

Talk About It
- Which part of Asaph's story do you most relate?

- Describe your personal sanctuary—the place you enjoy meeting with God. (If you don't yet have one, discuss some possibilities.)

- Can you identify a time when you were totally engaged in genuine worship?

- How does genuine worship affect your view of God? Your attention toward Him?

- What things tend to distract you from true worship?

- Identify a time you played the comparison game. What were the results?

- There are times it's important to share our inner struggles with others, and there are times we need to consider how it will affect someone if we unload everything. Asaph recognized this and used discernment in his situation. Will you commit to seeking God's discernment before unleashing inner turmoil on others?

Pray About It
Ask God to reveal specific things that tend to distract your focused attention on Him. As He brings these areas to your mind, seek His forgiveness and commit them to Him. Tell Him your desire to live a life of joyous worship and to squash the melancholy.

Chapter Four
Redirection from a Bad Road Trip

Talk About It
- What's the worst road trip you've ever experienced?

- Can you identify a time when you—like the two disciples in this chapter—bought into only the partial truth of a specific situation?

- Has defeat ever pushed you in the wrong direction? How far off course did you get?

- Share a time you focused on what you *saw* instead of what God *said*. How did that affect your relationship with Him?

- When in a tough situation, do you tend to continue in prayer as Adam and Amber did—or do you tend to take a few steps backward as Sierra did?

- What specifically can you do to consistently focus on what God has *said* instead of only what you can *see*?

Pray About It
Tell God that you desire to live by faith. Ask Him to help you keep your eyes focused on Him—even during the toughest of times—and to continue to seek His face when you can't see what's ahead.

Chapter Five
Redirection from Hopelessness

Talk About It
- Share the story of your name.

- Describe a circumstance that seemed to be hopeless and the way it affected you or your family.

- Many people, during difficult times, cling to the promises found in Psalm 23. Share some scriptures that comforted you during difficult times.
  -
  -

- We all know someone who's facing something difficult. What are some ways you can encourage him to realize there is hope?

Pray About It
Thank God for the promises He has made and kept. Praise Him specifically for Jesus—Immanuel—and the difference He is making in your life. Ask Him to remind you that He is always with you. Pray against hopelessness in your life and ask Him to use you to share the living Hope with those around you.

Chapter Six
Redirection from Worthlessness

Talk About It

• *Why me?* Have you ever said or thought that? Describe the situation.

• Share some labels you tend to identify with. (late, procrastinator, lazy, perfectionist, struggling, stern, divorced, etc.)

• Identify a time when you expected wrath and received grace instead.

• What would you need to change in order to enjoy the intimacy of sitting at the King's table every day?

• Go to YouTube and listen to Sidewalk Prophets sing "Come To the Table" and thank God for His invitation.

Pray About It

Spend some time giving your labels to God. Thank Him for never seeing you as a label but loving you in spite of your shortcomings. Ask Him to reveal anything in your life that's keeping you from intimacy with Him. Commit that area to Him and ask Him to help you deepen your relationship with Him.

Chapter Seven
Redirection from a Death Sentence

Talk About It

- You, too, may be experiencing something similar to Naaman or Kelly. Are you fighting the process like Naaman once did? Or are you submitting to the process?

- Are you finding it difficult to let go of something that God is trying to rid you of? (For Naaman, it was pride. What could it be in your life?)

- Describe a time you experienced God's blessing after going through a process that He guided you through?

- It all comes down to trust, doesn't it? What makes it difficult to fully trust Jesus in every area of your life?

Pray About It

Use this old hymn (by Louisa M.R. Stead and William J. Kirkpatrick) as your personal prayer:

'Tis so sweet to trust in Jesus,

Just to take Him at His Word;

Just to rest upon His promise;

Just to know, "Thus saith the Lord."

> Jesus, Jesus, how I trust Him!
>
> How I've proved Him o'er and o'er!
>
> Jesus, Jesus, precious Jesus!
>
> O for grace to trust Him more!

I'm so glad I learn to trust Thee,

Precious Jesus, Saviour, Friend;

And I know that Thou art with me,

Wilt be with me to the end.

Jesus, Jesus, how I trust Him!

How I've proved Him o'er and o'er!

> Jesus, Jesus, precious Jesus!
>
> O for grace to trust Him more!

Chapter Eight
Redirection from Shame

Talk About It

• Part of the dysfunction Tamar was caught up in began with the fact that David had several wives—and therefore several stepbrothers in Tamar's presence. We see lots of things that society has deemed normal—but they're not God's best. What are some of these things you see today?

• Have you mostly settled for Tamar's life . . . or are you mostly living a transformed life?

• Ron overcame his shame by allowing the Holy Spirit to use other Christians to speak truth into his life. Do you need to ask God to bring some godly people into your life to teach you the truth about who you are in Him?

• What's your reaction to the fact that God is singing over you?

• How does it make you feel to realize that you—not just your name, but the very essence of *you*—are engraved in the palm of His hand?

- The King wants to bring restoration, wholeness, healing and transformation to you. That's done only through the power of the Holy Spirit. What do you need to relinquish to allow the Holy Spirit complete control of your life (yes, this includes your self-esteem, your emotions, your past)?

- What will it take for you to refuse settling for less than God's best?

Pray About It

"Dear Jesus, I'm weary of being defined by shame. I hate my past. I've carried it around like a dark cloud hovering over my life. I don't want to live with this any longer. I want healing. I desire wholeness. I yearn for victory. And I know I can't get that by positive self-help talk. I need to be truly transformed by Your Holy Spirit. I want to be renewed inside and out.

So go ahead and break me. And then with Your loving hands, go ahead and reshape me in Your image. I give my past to You. I refuse to wear the shame label any longer. I'm Your child. And You love me more than I can imagine. Do in me whatever You need to do to make me whole. I'm asking this in Your powerful, healing name. Amen."

Chapter Nine
Redirection from Self

Talk About It

• What are some common areas in which you see people demanding instant gratification? What are the consequences of this?

• Identify some areas in your life that are easy to put before God.

• What specific things are easy for you to substitute in lieu of spiritual responsibilities? (Example: Reading the Bible is replaced by _____? Being more involved in ministry is replaced with _____?)

• Genesis chapters 32 and 33 show Jacob reaching out to Esau for restoration. He recognized his responsibility to make things right with his brother. Describe a time you sought forgiveness from someone you hurt. What was the end result?

• What changes are evident in one's life when he or she allows God to manifest the fruit of the Spirit?

• Go to YouTube and listen to TobyMac's song "Lose My Soul." What phrase stands out most to you in this song? Why?

Pray About It

Confess any self-centered attitudes to God. Be willing to relinquish trying to "work out" His plan for your life in your own way and your own timing. If you're not experiencing all the fruit of His Spirit, ask Him to reveal what's lacking and commit that area to God. Seek His guidance to reaching out to someone you may know who has made some poor choices and is hurting others in the process.

Chapter Ten
Redirection for Tomorrow

Talk About It

• Describe the situation and how old you were when you committed your life to Christ.

• Identify a time when the reality of Christ's presence was exceptionally powerful in your life.

• Sometimes it's difficult to get beyond our past. Discuss a time in your Christian walk when you found this to be true.

• Pinpoint an area of your life, with the Holy Spirit's help, that you're going to take steps to better influence your future.

• What does the statement, ". . . we have tomorrow, today" say about life with Jesus?

Pray About It

Spend some time giving any of your past to God that you've had difficulty letting go. Allow Him to heal those areas of your life. Thank Him for being willing to take your punishment on the Cross so you can experience real life. Ask Him to guide you to others who need to know this story and allow Him to use you to carry the good news.

Chapter Eleven
Redirection Becomes Sweet

Talk About It

• Describe a time when you invited Jesus directly into your situation (like Jamie did when she wanted her son home for Christmas) and the difference it made.

• If you're not seeing Christ's hand in your life, it could be due to not reading the Bible consistently. How often are you reading God's Word?

• Share a time (like Susie) that clinging to God's promises brought you great comfort during a time of grief or defeat.

• What's your personal response to these statements:
If you're going to have a relationship with Christ, you must be in the Written Word, because this is where the Living Word is revealed. This is where you learn of the resurrection power that the Holy Spirit offers to each one of us.

• Would you be willing to deepen your commitment to reading the Bible? Even if it's just one minute every day, you'll be surprised at the difference it will make in your life!

Pray About It

Let this old hymn be your prayer.

"The Solid Rock"
Words by Edward Mote

My hope is built on nothing less
than Jesus' blood and righteousness.
I dare not trust the sweetest frame,
but wholly lean on Jesus' name.
On Christ, the solid Rock I stand;
all other ground is sinking sand.
All other ground is sinking sand.

When darkness seems to hide His face,
I rest on His unchanging grace.
In ev'ry high and story gale,
my anchor holds within the veil.
On Christ, the solid Rock I stand;
all other ground is sinking sand.
All other ground is sinking sand.

His oath, His covenant, His blood,
 support me in the whelming flood.
When all around my soul gives way,
He then is all my Hope and Stay.
On Christ, the solid Rock I stand;
all other ground is sinking sand.
All other ground is sinking sand.

Chapter Twelve
Redirection Is a Wonderful Thing

Talk About It

• Describe something you used to do spiritually that you're not currently doing? (Bible study, sharing your faith, ministry involvement, etc.)

• How has it affected your spiritual cutting edge?

• What can you specifically do to get back your cutting edge? Are you willing to do it? What will need to change in your life to make this a reality?

• Grace Merrill shared a variety of things she does to keep the excitement in her quiet time (or devotional time) with God. Can you identify something you're doing to maintain your cutting edge? If not, would you consider using one of Grace's suggestions?

Pray About It

Ask God to help you serve Him with consistency. Tell Him you want to be spiritually alert and focused on Him. Let Him know that you're willing to commit your life to continued spiritual growth.

About the Authors

Rev. Susie Shellenberger, D.D., is an ordained minister and a tenured evangelist. (That's simply a fancy way of saying she talks. A LOT.) She's written 57 books (but says she hasn't read any of them), and bought a three-wheeled bicycle so she could take her two mini-Schnauzers Amos and Bentley for rides in the basket. She has appeared on the former Montel Williams Show, Fox News, HLN, and co-hosted a weekly live radio talk show "Life on the Edge, Live!"

Susie created BRIO Magazine for teen girls through Focus on the Family and served as editor for nearly 20 years. She's a former youth pastor and an ex high school speech, drama, creative writing and English teacher.

Susie has a master's degree in creative writing and a Doctor of Divinity. Susie is passionate about holiness and leads audiences into greater intimacy with Christ by combining Scripture with humor—delivering spiritual truth at lightning speed. To receive her free weekly email devotional blog, sign up through her Website: SusieShellenberger.com. To contact her for speaking engagements: susieshell@gmail.com.

In 1998, Billy Huddleston left a three-year youth pastorate near Chicago to be a full-time evangelist. As he spent time in youth ministry, he felt the Lord calling him to invest in the church the same way he was most encouraged as a believer. "Anything major that happened in my life," Billy explains, "happened at a revival."

Seeing how the Word impacted the direction of his life through revival services cultivated a zeal for others to experience the same. Today, Billy has a passion for seeing revival in the church and travels 48 weeks out of the year to preach the gospel of Jesus Christ to all denominations across the country. In addition to his travels, Billy hosts a radio program, "The Word In You," that airs weekly on stations across the nation.

In 2014, Billy debuted as an author with *Masterpiece,* a book he co-authored with Susie Shellenberger that encourages Believers to see themselves as Christ does. *Divine Redirection* is his second book.

Billy's music is played nationally on Southern Gospel Radio. He has been featured in the Christian Voice and Singing News magazines as well as charting on the Singing News Gospel Chart. Billy is known for delivering in-depth messages with an intensity and intelligence that aren't forgotten. He speaks at a wide variety of events across America spanning all denominations. You may contact and schedule Billy at: BillyHuddleston.com.